ARGUMENTS AGAINST G8

Arguments against G8

Edited by Gill Hubbard and David Miller

Pluto Press
London • Ann Arbor, MI

First published 2005 by Pluto Press
345 Archway Road, London N6 5AA
and 839 Greene Street, Ann Arbor, MI 48106

www.plutobooks.com

British Library Cataloguing in Publication Data
A catalogue record for this book is available from the British Library

ISBN 0 7453 2421 5 hardback
ISBN 0 7453 2420 7 paperback

Library of Congress Cataloging in Publication Data applied for

10 9 8 7 6 5 4 3 2 1

Designed and produced for Pluto Press by Curran Publishing Services, Norwich
Printed and bound in the European Union by Antony Rowe Ltd, Chippenham and
Eastbourne, England

Contents

Acknowledgements

Firstly, I would like to thank the Italians for organizing a massive mobilization against the summit of the G8 in Genoa in July 2001. All of you inspired me. If I had not been in Genoa I doubt that I would have got stuck in to mobilizing against the G8 in Gleneagles in 2005 as much as I have. Secondly, thanks to everyone around the world who stood together on 15 February 2003 to protest against Bush and Blair's war on Iraq. This war keeps me angry but your actions give me hope. Finally, thanks to Ian Mitchell – ex-miner – who never lets the bastards grind him down! I dedicate this book to you.

Gill Hubbard

I would like to acknowledge the millions of people all over the world who have seen through the lies of the great powers and have shown great imagination, perseverance, and above all courage in challenging the neo-liberal order. The great movements against neo-liberalism and against war reawaken the sense of a genuine international movement for justice and democracy. For so long, for all my adult life, democrats have been on the defensive in Scotland and Britain. The movement against war and against neo-liberalism has changed all that. There is a long road ahead, but at least it might lead forward instead of back.

Thanks are also due to Gill for taking on the bulk of the editorial work for this book. Thanks also to my colleagues on Spinwatch.org for their dedication in the face of what might over-optimistically be called a shoestring budget.

This book is for my children, Caitlin and Lewis, who have been neglected far too much by me in the process of its production (and the rest).

David Miller
February 2005

Abbreviations

AOA	(WTO) Agreement on Agriculture
CAP	Common Agricultural Policy
CMH	WHO Commission on Macroeconomics and Health
CSR	corporate social responsibility
DFID	Department for International Development
DTI	Department of Trade and Industry
ECLAC	Economic Commission for Latin America and the Caribbean
EPI	Economic Policy Institute
ERT	European Round Table of Industrialists
ESF	European Services Forum
FAO	Food and Agriculture Organization
FTAA	Free Trade Area of the Americas
GATS	General Agreement on Trade in Services
GATT	General Agreement on Tariffs and Trade
GDP	gross domestic product
HIPC	heavily indebted poor country
HRW	Human Rights Watch
ICC	International Chamber of Commerce
IFF	International Finance Facility
ILO	International Labour Organization
IMF	International Monetary Fund
IP	intellectual property
MAI	Multilateral Agreement on Investment
MSF	Médecins sans Frontières
NEPAD	New Partnership for Africa's Development

NGO	Non-Governmental Organization
OECD	Organisation for Economic Co-operation and Development
OPEC	Organization of the Petroleum Exporting Countries
OTA	Office of Technology Assessment
SSA	sub-Saharan Africa
TABD	Transatlantic Business Dialogue
TNC	transnational corporation
TRIPS	Trade-Related Aspects of Intellectual Property
UNCTAD	United Nations Conference on Trade and Development
WDM	World Development Movement
WEF	World Economic Forum
WHO	World Health Organization

About this book

This book is focused on the G8, an organization that is rather obscure, yet immensely powerful – the Group of Eight most industrialized nations. The G8 meet every year. Until recently they were able to meet in the open in the centre of large cities. The last time they came to Britain was in 1998, in the United Kingdom's second largest city of Birmingham. But since Genoa in 2001, when they were greeted with a huge protest and the Italian police murdered young Carlo Giuliani, they have been forced to meet in obscure and remote locations, easy to seal off and harder for protestors to get to.

In 2005 the G8 will meet in Gleneagles in Scotland. We have produced this book to spread the word that they are coming, and to provide a clear statement about who they are and why they should be opposed. This book is produced for the global justice movement and the global anti-war movement and for the millions more who might join them. It is also produced, in part, to show that these movements have coherent and sensible answers to the question of what is wrong with the G8. According to Tony Blair, globalization is inevitable. This book shows that his version of globalization – global inequality and environmental catastrophe – is not inevitable. Instead we show that a world of peace and environmental and social justice is both possible and necessary.

This book is a call to arms; a call to turn back the neo-liberal tide call, to reorder our world, to make another world possible. It is a sign of the strength and health of our movement that this is not the only book published recently in this vein. All over the world the rising tide of protest means there is a hunger for books, films and news that expose the poverty of the global political and economic system.

The introductory chapter by Gill Hubbard and David Miller introduces the severe problems afflicting the globe, the environmental catastrophe which faces us, global poverty, and the mania for privatizations, which cause and exacerbate these problems. The book deals with these questions by looking first at concentrated power. This opening chapter, by Noam Chomsky, sketches out the links between globalization and war. Chomsky argues that the 'masters of the universe', as the business press likes to describe our rulers, pursue war relentlessly. The only thing that can stop them, he concludes, is popular struggle.

Mark Curtis focuses on Britain and the G8. Blair is the 'host' of the G8 summit in Gleneagles in July 2005, and Curtis outlines the heavy responsibility of the British government for the inequality and poverty we see all around us. Most importantly he shows that behind the nice words about development and aid are the corporate interests that the Blair government attempts to camouflage under a patina of sincerity.

Colin Leys asks of the G8: where is your democratic legitimacy? He shows the staggering lack of democracy in the institutions of global and transnational government, and then outlines the neo-liberal assault on liberal democracy within Western nations.

Lindsey German exposes the link between capital and war. She notes that since the collapse of the Soviet Union, a 'new imperialism' dominated by the United States has arisen, and points to its Achilles heel: repression breeds resistance. Olivier Hoedeman discusses mounting corporate control across Europe, arguing that the European Union is now becoming a US-style 'lobbycracy' where corporations rule nakedly and directly. The G8 is a club for the most powerful nations to gain consensus about how best to pursue corporate interests, and as such, says

Hoedeman, a very significant obstacle to democracy and justice. Next, Emma Miller surveys the policies of the G8 nations on Africa and development. Africa is high on the agenda for the G8 summit in 2005, and Miller exposes the neo-liberal agendas embedded in the policies of all the members of the G8.

Section Two deals with some of the key issues highlighted by the global justice and anti-war movements. George Monbiot focuses on climate change, and how corporate interests undermine sensible policies with the aid of right-wing journalists, corporate front groups and pliant governments. Climate change is one of the big issues on the G8 agenda for 2005 but, Monbiot concludes, the omens for effective action in the face of the 'death of the planet' are not good.

Susan George examines the G8's collective article of faith: free trade. She argues that the freedom of the fox in the henhouse must be constrained, and that there must be democratic control of the world trade agenda.

The problems of trade are seen with particular force in the area of food security. Caroline Lucas lays out the crisis affecting world agriculture as small farmers go to the wall and biodiversity suffers under the influence of monocultures designed for export. In a world of more than enough food, millions continue to go hungry. She concludes that local food security is the only way to combat the problems of world hunger, which are exacerbated by trade-based export-oriented schemes.

Salma Yaqoob shows the connections between the war on terror, racism and neo-liberalism. She says that racism is central to the crises of migration thrown up by neo-liberalism, and that it is used to inculcate fear of Muslims in the pursuit of the war on terror. She shows that campaigns against the arms trade, Islamophobia and asylum are all connected by the centrality of racism to the strategies of the global elite.

Bob Crow suggests that 'liberal' is too nice a word for the

rulers of the planet. He discusses the global attack on workers' rights by examining the struggles in the United Kingdom against privatization, and in particular the struggles of the union he leads, the RMT. He calls for workers of all countries to unite to dismantle the neo-liberal edifice.

Tommy Sheridan focuses on poverty, and the obscene inequalities of wealth in the United Kingdom and elsewhere. He points to the need for massive redistribution of wealth if we are to abolish poverty. Vicki Clayton takes up the question of redistribution in her chapter on debt. She points out that the debt crisis has resulted in a massive transfer of wealth from the poor to the rich countries. She argues that the debt should be cancelled.

Ron Labonte, Ted Schrecker and David McCoy focus on the 'fatal indifference' of the G8 to the fate of sub-Saharan Africa. The obsession with the marketplace is at the cost of the people of Africa. They conclude that only a people-centred approach has any chance of tackling the health crises faced across sub-Saharan Africa.

In the concluding section Haidi Giuliani discusses how she decided early on in her life which side she was on. She tells how the murder of her son Carlo at the G8 summit in Genoa in 2001 affected her, and of her campaigns for truth and justice.

Sam Ashman interviewed a wide range of activists at the European Social Forum in London, and she presents their views on the next steps for the anti-war and global justice movements.

The book ends with an argument about the root causes of the environmental and social catastrophes of our time. Everywhere we look, the same social system is at the root of our contemporary problems. This chapter makes an argument that not all in the movement will agree with, but it does stake out the need for us to stay united if we are to move forward.

This book was produced against a very tight deadline, and we thank all the contributors who have helped to make it possible.

As we were about to go to press, the tsunami happened. It still remains unclear exactly how many people have perished but at the time of writing it had reached well over 200,000. While this was a natural disaster caused by a movement of the earth's plates, its consequences were not. These have been well documented elsewhere.[1] There was no early warning system in place in the Indian ocean; mangrove forests, which act as a natural barrier to the sea, had been cut down to pave the way for the tourist industry and aquaculture; the areas worst hit were poor and unlike more affluent parts of the world prone to tsunamis and earthquakes (for example, Japan and Hawaii) people's homes and places of work had not been built to withstand such natural disasters.

Ordinary people around the world watched in horror and donated millions to help the victims. This was not charity but an act of genuine solidarity. Meanwhile the leaders of the eight richest countries in the world stood by impotent. Tony Blair, president of the G8, remained on holiday in Egypt rather than return to tackle one of the biggest global disasters in 50 years. Blair only increased aid when it became clear that people were spontaneously donating on an unprecedented scale. It has not gone unnoticed that Bush and Blair could quickly find money for war and death in Iraq but not for rebuilding people's lives in the areas affected by the tsunami. The ability of the G8 to handle global disasters has been put to the test. They are failing and failing badly.

DM and GH

NOTE

1   Ungpakorn, Giles Ji (2005) ' A "natural" disaster made worse by the profit system', *Socialist Worker*, report from Bangkok, Thailand, 8 January;

Moonesinghe, Vinod (2005) 'System that keeps us poor made the tsunami so lethal', *Socialist Worker*, report from Colombo, Sri Lanka, 8 January, <http://www.socialistworker.co.uk/article.php4?article_id=5101>; Pilger, John (2005) 'The other, man-made tsunami', 7 January <http://www.zmag.org/Sustainers/Content/2005-01/07pilger.cfm>.

Introduction
Barbarism Inc.

Gill Hubbard and David Miller

George You can literally watch the world's water supply dripping away moment by moment.

Ruth But that's just someone's opinion.

George That's not an opinion it's a scientific hypothesis. Let's just say they're half right, which chances say they are. But even if they're only half right we're not doing any of the things we should be doing in order to prevent it, much less reverse the trend.

Ruth But it's all so pessimistic. If it happens we'll die. In the meantime can't we be happy?

George Happy?

(Excerpt from episode of American TV series
Six Feet Under)

Replace the world's water supply with any other natural resource – oil, rainforest, soil, fish stocks, minerals, fossil fuel, wildlife, the ozone shield – and the picture stays the same. The trajectory of the global capitalist economy at the beginning of the twenty-first century is on a collision course with nature. Some of us used to joke that if corporations could bottle and sell the air that we breathe they would do it. Well, now nobody is laughing.

Our ecological system is in peril. Scientists estimate that a reduction of 70 per cent of greenhouse gas emissions over this century is necessary to prevent the worst effects of climate change, including flooding, hurricanes and droughts. Yet the Kyoto pact, which is part of the United Nations Framework on Climate Change, only requires developed countries to reduce greenhouse emissions by 5.2 per cent by 2012. And the United States, which is the world's biggest polluter – spurting out 5,795.6 million metric tonnes of carbon dioxide[1] – has refused to sign the pact.

Climate change with its calamitous consequences is just one of the issues that the eight richest countries in the world have failed to tackle. The summit of these eight countries – Britain, Canada, France, Germany, Italy, Japan, Russia and the United States – will meet (or by the time that you read this book, will have met) in July 2005 in Scotland. The G8 (in its original form as the G6) met for the first time in 1975. They have had 30 years to alleviate the misery and poverty endured by people in some of the poorest parts of the world. Yet at the beginning of the twenty-first century:

- A child every 15 seconds dies from lack of safe water.
- Most of the estimated 30,000 daily human deaths are preventable. Of the 20 countries with the highest child mortality rates, 19 are in Africa, the only exception being Afghanistan.
- Half of the people living in sub-Saharan Africa are living on less than a dollar a day, which is half the level of subsidy given to European cows.
- One billion people – approximately one-third of the world's urban dwellers and a sixth of all humanity – live in slums.
- While at least a billion people on the planet subsist on the equivalent of a dollar a day or less, the concentration of

wealth among a handful of people at the top has set new records. In March 2004 *Forbes* magazine listed a record 587 individuals and family units worth US$1 billion or more, an increase from 476 in 2003. The combined wealth of billionaires also reached record levels – a staggering US$1.9 trillion, an increase of US$500 billion in just one year.

These figures suggest that the G8 either have a penchant for keeping the majority of the world's population in a perpetual state of impoverishment, or head a global system that is out of control. How much longer should we let them decide the fate of our planet?

The G8 have consistently imposed a neo-liberal economic model that benefits the rich and powerful at the expense of the most destitute people in the world. This type of economics is characterized by privatization, deregulation and trade liberalization.

Take the case of trade liberalization. An increase in international trade for the world's poorest countries has not led to any real reduction in poverty in these countries. The United Nations Conference on Trade and Development reported that the majority of people in countries that opened up their markets for free trade are still surviving on less than US$1 a day. In other words, the people who gain most from relaxing import and export controls in the developing world are the multinationals.

The G8 continue to demand that poor countries open up their borders so that transnational corporations can swoop down and bleed public services dry. Like vultures, the corporations circle over the developing world, waiting to feed off the profits. The International Monetary Fund (IMF) and World Bank insist that to qualify for debt relief or loans poor countries must privatize public utilities including water, gas, electricity, transport, hospitals and schools. Privatization has increased the costs of these essential services, which means that poor people can no longer afford them. Privatization of public services has clearly exacerbated the effects of poverty in many developing countries. Take the case of sub-Saharan Africa. The Organisation for Economic Co-operation and Development drew the following conclusion on the privatization of public utilities:

> In the absence of proper regulation, profit-maximising behaviour has led privatised companies to keep investments below the necessary levels, with the result that rural communities and the urban poor were further marginalised in terms of access to electric power and water supply.[2]

UK corporations are conspicuous in the scramble for African public services. For example, Johannesburg City Council in a public-private partnership with Northumbrian Water and its French parent Suez Lyonnaise des Eaux has recently installed pre-paid water meters. Those who cannot afford to pay are left with no other choice than to draw their water from dirty rivers. These people then become most at risk of succumbing to life-threatening ailments such as cholera and diarrhoea. Residents are resisting by ripping up pipelines.[3]

Perhaps it is not surprising that UK companies have their finger in the privatization pie. Despite evidence showing that privatization has nothing to offer poor people but more hardship and misery, the UK government has championed the privateers by investing heavily in an international privatization programme. According to War on Want,[4] the Department for International Development (DFID) has used its aid budget to usher in privatization. Consultants from accountancy firms such as PricewaterhouseCoopers and Ernst and Young, with their beady eyes on services ripe for privatization, line up to receive their reward from the government aid budget. For example the Adam Smith Institute, which was the British think tank behind privatization of public services in the 1980s, has received over £34 million from DFID's aid budget in the past six years for projects including running pro-privatization propaganda campaigns in southern Africa.[5]

Much closer to home, public services are being privatized without any evidence to suggest that this will lead to improvements. Indeed, all evidence points in the other direction. We only have to look at the British train service as proof that privatization has been a disaster. Since privatization, this key part of our transport infrastructure has had escalating costs, deteriorating performance and a poor safety record.[6]

But it is not just the enforced privatization agenda that is responsible for so much human hardship. Neo-liberal economists from the pulpits of the World Bank and IMF also lay down strict budgetary constraints on public spending as a condition of receiving aid and loans. In doing so, they prevent countries in the developing world from hiring doctors, nurses and health workers and purchasing much needed medicines to fight diseases such as HIV/AIDS.

An estimated 40 million people in the world have HIV/AIDS, and 28 million of them live in sub-Saharan Africa. More children die in sub-Saharan Africa now than a decade ago. One in six children in sub-Saharan Africa dies before the age of five compared with one in 143 in industrialized countries. This is largely as a result of HIV/AIDS. Children who do survive are often orphaned. The United Nations estimates that 11 million children in sub-Saharan Africa have lost at least one parent to the disease, and predicts that by the end of the decade there will be 20 million.

The issue of HIV/AIDS did not even reach 2004's G8 agenda; instead, it was discussed for two hours over a 'working lunch'. The G8 endorsed coordinated international research for an HIV/AIDS vaccine, yet the United Nations estimates that Africa alone needs US$10 billion to fight HIV/AIDS each year. The World AIDS Campaign is still waiting for the G8 to honour the United Nations Global AIDS Agreement that it signed three years ago. Those people with HIV/AIDS need the money now to pay for the drugs that will keep them alive today – tomorrow may be too late.

The landscape of Africa is receiving particular attention in 2005. Immediately after being handed the presidency of the G8, Tony Blair announced a Commission for Africa. Africa has debts of £171 billion. Its products account for only 2 per cent of world trade. The threat of famine in countries such as Ethiopia is twice as bad now as it was 20 years ago, when millions of people around the world gave money to Band Aid and Live Aid while rock stars played to audiences in Britain and the United States. The song 'Feed the world' became an instant Christmas hit. So what has Tony Blair got in store for the people of Africa?

Despite his declaring himself the saviour of Africa, weapons are being sold with the blessing of the Labour government on an unprecedented scale. For instance, the government of South Africa is purchasing warships and military aircraft to the value of US$4.8 billion from the UK and other European suppliers.[7] The UK has also sold arms to Egypt, Ghana, Kenya, Sierra Leone and Zambia.

Tony Blair also seems to think that privatizing public services is the answer to many of Africa's problems. In 2002, DFID created the Emerging Africa Infrastructure Fund in order to provide finance to private companies that seek to own and control public services in African countries.

And since the Blair government has been in office, Britain has still not fulfilled the promise made over 30 years ago to the United Nations to increase aid to 0.7 per cent of national income. (Britain currently gives 0.34 per cent, which is approximately £3.83 billion.) This means that Britain owes developing countries, many of them African, a staggering £10 billion in aid.[8] On the other hand, Britain reserved £3.8 billion for the Iraq war, the costs of which are still rising. An opinion poll reported in the *Guardian* shows that 60 per cent of the British public say that money spent on the Iraq war would have been better spent on tackling poverty in poor countries.[9]

The G8 expound the gospel of globalization. Like a phalanx they march across the globe, pushing into the gutter anyone or anything that stands in their way. The term 'globalization' has a specific meaning. It is the accelerated integration of capital, production of goods and services, and markets on a global scale. Globalization is a process that is driven by the logic of corporations competing with one another for natural and human labour resources, and for markets in which to sell goods and services. This logic extends to rivalries between nation states, which is why globalization is also characterized by war.

Globalization has had three main phases. The first phase lasted from the early nineteenth century until the outbreak of the First World War. This was characterized by largely unlimited opportunities to exploit resources and markets worldwide. This was, of course, only after countries had been colonized, which meant murder, torture, displacement and the subjugation of local populations across all continents. Britain was the supreme superpower in this first phase. Through the double standard of protecting its own corporations and markets while at the same time demanding free and open trade from other countries, Britain's geopolitical reach was far and wide.

The second phase lasted until about the 1970s. This was a period characterized by the dominance of national economies, and an international economy with strong constraints on trade and capital flows. Keynesian economic policies regulated capitalism both domestically and internationally, following mass action by the working class in Western countries and the experience of the Second World War. This meant that corporations were restricted in their ability to own and control resources and markets within different countries. Import and export controls were the norm, and nation states were able to control what went in and out of their borders.

The third phase started in the late 1970s and continues today. This phase is marked by the ideology of neo-liberalism. Constraints on financial speculation and trade are being rapidly eradicated. This means that corporations are attempting to remove any regulation that gets in their way, including laws on safety of medicines and chemicals, environmental standards and workers' rights. Thus neo-liberalism amounts to a direct attack on the abilities of nation states to decide who owns and controls the resources that lie within their geographical boundaries. Neo-liberalism also poses a formidable challenge to trade unions and to the welfare state, because it is largely these bodies that have managed to offer at least some protection from the unfettered effects of corporate profiteering. Without a welfare safety net people are left to fend for themselves once they are thrown on the scrap heap.

There are three interconnected international bodies that are forcing through globalization in this third phase: The IMF, the World Bank, and the World Trade Organization (WTO). Between them they aim to establish 'global governance' based on the principles of unchecked financial flows and speculation on the stock markets, free trade and privatization.

The purpose of the IMF is to make sure that financial speculation, gambling on currencies and the buying and selling of corporate shares, can go on unchecked. It wants this free-for-all to take place irrespective of the consequences. For example, when the world's gamblers started a run on the baht, the Thai currency, it precipitated the Asian financial crisis of 1997. In a matter of weeks over a million people in Thailand and 21 million people in Indonesia were pushed below the poverty line.

Like grand schoolmasters, the IMF and World Bank tell governments in the developing world what they should do with their economies. The developing countries are being taught to abide by 'structural adjustment programmes', which are now disingenuously called 'poverty reduction strategies'. If governments refuse to do as they are told, detention for the pupil is severe. The IMF and World Bank have refused to provide aid and loans to these countries. In the past, debt relief was denied to seven heavily indebted countries because they had not abided by IMF and World Bank neo-liberal economic programmes. It is not from lack of money that members of the G8 refuse to cancel Third World debt, it is because debt can be used as a way of coercing developing countries to adopt neo-liberal economic practices.

Ethiopia has been a model pupil of the IMF for a number of years. The purpose of the 'Sustainable Development Poverty Reduction Programme' drawn up for the country was to build a free market economic system, yet the IMF admits that things have not been going too well recently. In its 2004 Annual Report[10] the IMF has acknowledged that 'conditions have probably worsened for the majority'. One of the four pillars of the development strategy was 'Agricultural Development Led Industrialization' (ADLI). So how well has the agriculture sector fared under the tutelage of the IMF? The collapse of world coffee prices has 'shattered livelihoods', and widely fluctuating prices for crops have created enormous hardship for farmers. This is how the IMF describe what has happened to farmers:

> Bumper crops in earlier years drove down food prices, with catastrophic effects on farmers' income. Consequently, many farmers could not repay their debt, and did not have the means to purchase and apply modern inputs to this year's crops.

In other words, ADLI has been a total disaster. Yet, the IMF continues to preach that a free market economy is the panacea to Ethiopia's problems.

The purpose of the WTO is to establish free trade so that corporations can do what they want and go where they want without anything or anyone standing in their way. There will be no barbed wire fences or border police blocking the path of transnational corporations. It is the WTO that is imposing Trade-Related Intellectual Property Rights (TRIPS). This is the intellectual equivalent of armed robbery. Our human genes and basic foodstuffs are being patented. Patenting has meant, for example, that the production of cheaper, generic drugs that would keep people with HIV/AIDS alive is being blocked. In other words, pharmaceutical profits are protected and the poor and sick are paying the price.

The 'Battle of Seattle' in 1999 outside the WTO is seen as the beginning of a wave of global protest against the neo-liberal project, although a wave of protest in the developing world had preceded it, from 1994 onwards. It was not only the anti-capitalists who were compelled to protest in Seattle. Governments from developing countries were also outraged by the hypocrisy of the eight richest nations in the world. For example, while they were expected to open up their country's borders to corporations from abroad, and remove support given to key sectors of the economy, the United States was busy propping up its own agricultural and steel industries through massive subsidies. The United States took a position of 'Don't do what I do, but do as I say.' In other words, it was all right for the United States to flout the free trade rules but not for others.

Protesters outside the WTO in Seattle were there to oppose corporate power and more. They detested the likes of Gap and Nike for exploiting workers in the developing world, and they hated the fact that corporations that were responsible for cutting down rainforests and for polluting the planet were to be given even more powers.

The crisis of legitimacy of the neo-liberal project was exposed again in Genoa at the G8 summit in 2001. As hundreds of thousands of demonstrators took to the streets to declare that another world is possible, the most powerful leaders of the world met behind huge wire fences, protected by armed personnel. The murder by police of Carlo Giuliani, a young Genoese man in his twenties, was a blunt and brutal reminder that violence could and would be meted out on a social movement that was predominantly clad in T-shirts and jeans. But Genoa was also a reminder of the power and strength of this social movement. Since Genoa, the G8 has kept away from meeting in major urban conurbations.

Further witness to the power and seriousness of this social movement is given by the tens of thousands who have gathered to discuss, debate and demonstrate at European and World Social Forums (30,000 in Florence 2002, 60,000 in Paris 2003, 20,000 in London 2004, and over 100,000 at the World Social Forum in Mumbai in 2004). Although people spoke in different tongues the language was the same – it was a language that spoke clearly against war and neo-liberalism. Activists came together to fight for a 'different world'.

The storm clouds gathering over the corporate-driven glob-alization agenda on the streets of Seattle and Genoa have been joined by a hurricane – the anti-war movement. The war and occupation of Iraq has already cost thousands of lives and caused untold human misery. The leading medical journal *The Lancet* gives 100,000 deaths as a conservative estimate for the people of Iraq alone. The warmongers within the G8 have witnessed huge protests against their bloodshed. The aftermath of 9/11, far from stopping the anti-capitalist movement in its tracks (which was predicted by the majority of political commentators), has seen a fusion of the struggles against neo-liberalism and war. It was in Florence at the European Social Forum in November 2002 and then at the World Social Forum in Porto Alegre in January 2003 that it was agreed to mobilize across the world on 15 February against the then impending war on Iraq. Millions took to the streets on that day.

The relationship between neo-liberalism and war has never been starker than in the war against Iraq. This war, which was led by the United States with Britain obediently following, has compounded the crisis of legitimacy of global capitalism in at least three ways. The war and occupation of Iraq showed what the 'Project for a New American Century' actually means in practice. It means control of oil supplies and it means profits for US corporations. Nowhere has this been more blatant than in awarding the main business contracts for the so-called 'rebuilding' of Iraq to US corporations linked to the Bush gang, such as Bechtel and Halliburton. UK corpora-tions were left to peck the crumbs off the table after the hawks had had their fill.

Bush and Blair alleged that this war was about bringing democracy to the people of Iraq, but what it has done is to drive the quest for democracy even further away from the hands of the Iraqi people. How can you have a democracy when there are no free and fair elections? How can you call it democracy when foreign troops occupy the country? How can it be a democracy when the whole economy is owned by a foreign power?

This war has also led millions to question the type of democracy that is much closer to home. British democracy, which is one of the oldest in the world, is now in the spotlight. Blair used the fact that Saddam Hussein had weapons of mass destruction that could be fired in 45 minutes as a pretext for supporting Bush's war against Iraq. Some people have called this 'spin'; others have referred to it as a 'misrepresentation of the truth', or as 'misleading information', a 'half-truth' or 'deliberately ambiguous'. But let us call it what it really is – a lie. Blair did lie. He lied in parliament and he lied to the people of Britain – and not just about the 45 minutes claim. He is lying still.[11]

Finally, the war and occupation of Iraq have brought in a wave of horrors. The torture and abuse of Iraqi prisoners demonstrated to the whole world that the elites in the United States and Britain didn't give a damn about the Geneva Convention and cared even less about Iraqi lives. Nagem Salam interviewed a former Abu Ghraib female detainee who was arrested by US forces on 14 September 2003 and detained in Ba'qouba, Tikrit, Abu Ghraib and the Tesfirat transfer station.[12] She describes how 14 Iraqi men were treated in Abu Ghraib:

> The soldiers made them all stand on one leg, then they kicked them to make them fall to the ground.... The soldiers also made all the men lay on the ground, face down, spread their legs, then men and women soldiers alike kicked the detainees between their legs.... I can still remember their screaming.... Every day, morning and evening, I saw people tortured and humiliated in the corridor in front of my cell.

And people still remain incarcerated in Guantanamo Bay without recourse to a fair trial. With hands tied behind their backs and blindfolded, they sit isolated in cages not knowing their fate.

Given the failed history of the G8 it is no surprise that people have protested when they meet. The leaders of the eight richest countries in the world may take their photo-opportunities, but there are millions of us ready to point out their hypocrisy and reveal the G8 for what they really are: a rich cabal trying to disguise themselves as pious philanthropists. We will not be fooled. This is why at the Assembly of Social Movements, which was attended by over 1,000 people representing individuals and organizations from different European countries on the last day of the European Social Forum in London 2004, there was agreement to 'mobilize massively' for protest during the summit of the G8 in Gleneagles, Scotland 2005.

NOTES

1   Energy Information Administration, 2002
     <http://www.eia.doe.gov/oiaf/1605/ggrpt/carbon.html>, accessed 22 October 2004.
2   Barthélemy, J, Kauffman, C, Valfort, M and Wegner, L (2004) *Privatisation in Sub-Saharan Africa: Where do we stand?* Organisation for Economic Co-operation and Development, Paris.
3   Monbiot, George (2004) 'Exploitation on tap', *Guardian*, 19 October.
4   War on Want (2004) *Profiting from Poverty: Privatisation consultants, DFID and public services*, War on Want, London.
5   Monbiot, George (2004) 'On the edge of lunacy', *Guardian*, 6 January
     <http://www.monbiot.com/archives/2004/01/06/
     on-the-edge-of-lunacy/>.
6   Catalyst (2004) *Renaissance delayed? New Labour and the railways*, Catalyst, London
     <http://www.rmt.org.uk/C2B/document_tree/
     ViewADocument.asp?ID=264&CatID=40>

7   Campaign Against the Arms Trade (2003) *The South African Deal,*
     Campaign Against the Arms Trade, London.
8   WorldVision (2004) *UK in Top 10 Countries Contributing to $344
     Billion Aid Black Hole*, 14 June <www.worldvision.org.uk>.
9   Shifrin, Tash (2004) 'War money "better spent on tackling poverty"',
     Guardian, Tuesday 8 June
     <http://politics.guardian.co.uk/iraq/story/0,12956,1234104,00.html>.
10   IMF (2004) *Poverty Reduction Strategy Paper, Annual Progress Report*,
     12 February
     <http://www.imf.org/external/pubs/ft/scr/2004/cr0437.pdf>.
11   Miller, David (ed.) (2004) *Tell Me Lies: Propaganda and media distor-
     tion in the attack on Iraq*, Pluto, London.
12   Salam, Nagem (2004) *A Tree with No Roots: One Iraqi woman's story*,
     14 June
     <http://www.islamonline.net/english/In_Depth/
     Iraq_Aftermath/2004/06/article_04.shtml>.

Section One
Concentrated Power

1 Globalization and war[1]

Noam Chomsky

It is hardly exciting news that we live in a world of conflict and confrontation. There are lots of dimensions and complexities, but in recent years, lines have been drawn fairly sharply. To oversimplify, but not too much, one of the participants in the conflict is concentrated power centres, state and private, closely interlinked. The other is the general population, worldwide. In old-fashioned terms, it would have been called 'class war'.

Concentrated power pursues the war relentlessly, and very self-consciously. Government documents and publications of the business world reveal that they are mostly vulgar Marxists, with values reversed of course. They are also frightened – back to seventeenth-century England in fact. They realize that the system of domination is fragile, that it relies on disciplining the population by one or another means. There is a desperate search for such means: in recent years, Communism, crime, drugs, terrorism, and others. Pretexts change, policies remain rather stable. Sometimes the shift of pretext along with continuity of policy is dramatic and takes real effort to miss: immediately after the collapse of the USSR, for example.[2] They naturally grasp every opportunity to press their agenda forward: 9/11 is a typical case. Crises make it possible to exploit fear and concern to demand that the adversary be submissive, obedient, silent, distracted, while the powerful use the window of opportunity to pursue their own favoured programmes with even greater intensity. These programmes vary, depending on the society: in the more brutal states, escalation of repression and terror; in societies where the population has won more freedom, measures to impose discipline while shifting wealth and power even more to their own hands. It is easy to list examples around the world in the past few months.

Their victims should certainly resist the predictable exploitation of crisis, and should focus their own efforts, no less relentlessly, on the primary issues that remain much as they were before: among them, increasing militarism, destruction of the environment, and a far-reaching assault against democracy and freedom, the core of 'neo-liberal' programmes.

The ongoing conflict is symbolized by the World Social Forum and the World Economic Forum in New York. The WEF – to quote the national US press – is a gathering of 'movers and shakers', the 'rich and famous', 'wizards from around the world', 'government leaders and corporate executives, ministers of state and of God, politicians and pundits' who are going to 'think deep thoughts' and address 'the big problems confronting humankind'. A few examples are given, for example, 'How do you inject moral values into what we do?' Or a panel entitled 'Tell me what you eat,' led by the 'reigning prince of the New York gastronomic scene', whose elegant restaurants will be 'mobbed by forum participants'. There is also mention of an 'anti-forum' in Brazil. These are 'the freaks who assemble to protest the meetings of the World Trade Organization'. One can learn more about the freaks from a photo of a scruffy looking guy, with face concealed, writing 'world killers' on a wall.

At their 'carnival,' as it is described, the freaks are throwing stones, writing graffiti, dancing and singing about a variety of boring topics that are unmentionable, at least in the United

States: investment, trade, financial architecture, human rights, democracy, sustainable development, Brazilian-African relations, GATS and other marginal issues. They are not 'thinking deep thoughts' about 'big problems'; that is left to the wizards of Davos in New York.

The infantile rhetoric, I presume, is a sign of well-deserved insecurity.

The freaks at the 'anti-forum' in Porto Alegre are defined as being 'opposed to globalization', a propaganda weapon we should reject with scorn. 'Globalization' just means international integration. No sane person is 'anti-globalization'. That should be particularly obvious for the labour movement and the left; the term 'international' is not exactly unknown in their history. In fact, the WSF is the most exciting and promising realization of the hopes of the left and popular movements, from their modern origins, for a true international, which will pursue a programme of globalization concerned with the needs and interests of people, rather than of illegitimate concentrations of power. These, of course, want to appropriate the term 'globalization', and to restrict it to *their* peculiar version of international integration, concerned with their own interests, those of people being incidental. With this ridiculous terminology in place, those who seek a sane and just form of globalization can be labelled 'anti-globalization', derided as primitivists who want to return to the stone age, to harm the poor, and subjected to other terms of abuse with which we are familiar.

The wizards of Davos modestly call themselves the 'international community', but perhaps we should adopt the term used by the world's leading business journal: 'the masters of the universe'.[3] Since the masters profess to be admirers of Adam Smith, we might expect them to abide by his account of their behaviour, though he only called them 'the masters of mankind' – that was before the space age.

Smith was referring to the 'principal architects of policy' of his day, the merchants and manufacturers of England, who made sure that their own interests are 'most peculiarly attended to' however 'grievous' the impact on others, including the people of England. At home and abroad, they pursue 'the vile maxim of the masters of mankind': 'all for ourselves and nothing for other people'. It should hardly surprise us that today's masters honour the same 'vile maxim'. At least they try, though they are sometimes impeded by the freaks – the 'great beast', to borrow a term used by the Founding Fathers of American democracy to refer to the unruly population that did not comprehend that the primary goal of government is 'to protect the minority of the opulent from the majority', as the leading Framer of the Constitution explained in the debates of the Constitutional Convention.

I will return to these matters, but first a few words about 'a world without war'. We cannot say much about human affairs with any confidence, but sometimes it is possible. We can, for example, be fairly confident that either there will be a world without war or there won't be a world – at least, a world inhabited by creatures other than bacteria and beetles, with some scattering of others. The reason is familiar: humans have developed means of destroying themselves, and much else, and have come dangerously close to using them for half a century. Furthermore, the leaders of the civilized world are now dedicated to enhancing these dangers to survival, in full awareness of what they are doing, at least if they read the reports of their own intelligence agencies and respected strategic analysts, including many who strongly favour the race to destruction. Still more ominous, the plans are developed and implemented on grounds that are rational within the dominant framework of ideology and values, which ranks survival well below 'hegemony', the goal pursued by advocates of these programmes, as they often state quite frankly.

Wars over water, energy and other resources are not unlikely in the future, with consequences that could be devastating. In substantial measure, however, wars have had to do with the imposition of the system of nation states, an unnatural social formation that typically has to be instituted by violence. That is a primary reason that Europe was the most savage and brutal part of the world for many centuries, meanwhile conquering most of the world. European efforts to impose state systems in conquered territories are the source of most conflicts underway right now, after the collapse of the formal colonial system. Europe's own favourite sport of mutual slaughter had to be called off in 1945, when it was realized that the next time the game was played would be the last. Another prediction that we can make with fair confidence is that there will be no war among great powers; the reason is that if the prediction turns out to be wrong, there will be no one around to care to tell us.

Furthermore, popular activism within the rich and powerful societies has had a civilizing effect. The 'movers and shakers' can no longer undertake the kinds of long-term aggression that were options before, as when the United States attacked South Vietnam 40 years ago, smashing much of it to pieces before significant popular protest developed. Among the many civilizing effects of the ferment of the 1960s was broad opposition to large-scale aggression and massacre, reframed in the ideological system as unwillingness to accept casualties among the armed forces ('the Vietnam syndrome'). The Reaganites had to resort to international terrorism instead of invading Central America directly, on the Kennedy-Johnson model. The same changes explain the intelligence review of the incoming Bush-I administration in 1989, warning that in conflicts against 'much weaker enemies' – the only kind it makes sense to confront – the United States must 'defeat them decisively and rapidly', or the campaign will lose 'political support', understood to be thin. Wars since have kept to that pattern, and the scale of protest and dissent has steadily increased. So there are changes, of a mixed nature.

When pretexts vanish, new ones have to be concocted to control the great beast, while traditional policies are continued, adapted to new circumstances. That was already becoming clear 20 years ago. It was hard not to recognize that the Soviet enemy was facing internal problems and might not be a credible threat much longer. That is, presumably, part of the reason that the Reagan administration, 20 years ago, declared that the 'war on terror' would be the focus of US foreign policy, particularly in Central America and the Middle East, the main source of the plague spread by 'depraved opponents of civilization itself' in a 'return to barbarism in the modern age', as Administration moderate George Shultz explained, also warning that the solution is violence, avoiding 'utopian, legalistic means like outside mediation, the World Court, and the United Nations'. We need not tarry on how the war was waged in those two regions, and elsewhere, by the extraordinary network of proxy states and mercenaries – an 'axis of evil', to borrow a more up-to-date term.

It is a fair guess that the 'war on terror' will serve as a pretext for intervention and atrocities in coming years, not just by the United States; Chechnya is only one of a number of examples. The 'war on terror' has, of course, been the focus of a huge literature, during the first phase in the 1980s and since it was redeclared in the past few months. One interesting feature of the flood of commentary, then and now, is that we are not told what 'terror' is. What we hear, rather, is that this is a vexing and complex question. That is curious: there are straightforward definitions in official US documents. A simple one takes terror to be the 'calculated use of violence or threat of violence to attain goals that are political, religious, or ideological in nature...'. That seems appropriate enough, but it cannot be used, for two good reasons. One is that it also defines official policy, called 'counterinsurgency' or 'low-intensity conflict'. Another is that it yields all the wrong answers, facts too obvious to review though suppressed with remarkable efficiency.

The problem of finding a definition of 'terror' that will exclude the most prominent cases is indeed vexing and complex. But fortunately, there is an easy solution: define 'terror' as terror that *they* carry out against *us*. A review of the scholarly literature on terror, the media and intellectual journals will show that this usage is close to exceptionless, and that any departure from it elicits impressive tantrums. Furthermore, the practice is probably universal: the generals in South America were protecting the population from terror directed from outside, just as the Japanese were in Manchuria and the Nazis in occupied Europe. If there is an exception, I haven't found it.

Let us return to 'globalization', and the linkage between it and the threat of war, perhaps terminal war.

The version of 'globalization' designed by the masters of the universe has very broad elite support, not surprisingly, as do the so-called 'free trade agreements' – what the business press, more honestly, sometimes calls 'free investment agreements'. Very little is reported about these issues, and crucial information is simply suppressed. For example, after a decade, the position of the US labour movement on NAFTA, and the conforming conclusions of Congress's own Research Bureau (the Office of Technology Assessment, OTA), have yet to be reported outside of dissident sources.[4] And the issues are off the agenda in electoral politics. There are good reasons. The masters know well that the public will be opposed if information becomes available. They are fairly open when addressing one another, however. Thus a few years ago, under enormous public pressure, Congress rejected the 'fast track' legislation that grants the President authority to enact international economic arrangements with Congress permitted to vote 'Yes' (or, theoretically, 'No') with no discussion, and the public uninformed. Like other sectors of elite opinion, the *Wall Street Journal* was distraught over the failure to undermine democracy. But it explained the problem: opponents of these Stalinist-style measures have an 'ultimate weapon', the general population, which must therefore be kept in the dark.[5] That is very important, particularly in the more democratic societies, where dissidents can't simply be jailed or assassinated, as in the leading recipients of US military aid, such as El Salvador, Turkey and Colombia, to list the recent and current world champions (Israel–Egypt aside).

One might ask why public opposition to 'globalization' has been so high for many years. That seems strange, in an era when it has led to unprecedented prosperity, so we are constantly informed, particularly in the United States, with its 'fairytale economy'. Through the 1990s, the United States has enjoyed 'the greatest economic boom in America's history – and the world's', Anthony Lewis wrote in the *New York Times* a year ago,[6] repeating the standard refrain from the left end of the admissible spectrum. It is conceded that there are flaws: some have been left behind in the economic miracle, and we good-hearted folk must do something about that. The flaws reflect a profound and troubling dilemma: the rapid growth and prosperity brought by 'globalization' has as a concomitant growing inequality, as some lack the skills to enjoy the wondrous gifts and opportunities.

The picture is so conventional that it may be hard to realize how little resemblance it has to reality, facts that have been well known right through the miracle. Until the brief late-1990s boomlet (which scarcely compensated for earlier stagnation or decline for most people), per capita growth in the United States in the 'roaring 1990s' was about the same as the rest of the industrial world, lower than in the first 25 post-war years before so-called 'globalization', and vastly lower than the war years, the greatest economic boom in American history, under a semi-command economy. How then can the conventional picture be so radically different from uncontroversial facts? The answer is simplicity itself. For a small sector of the society, the 1990s really were a grand economic boom. That sector happens to include those who tell others the joyous news. And they cannot be accused of dishonesty. They have no reason to doubt what they are saying. They read it all the time in the journals for which they write, and it accords with their personal experience: it is true of the people they meet in editorial offices, faculty clubs, elite conferences like the one the wizards are now attending, and the elegant restaurants where they dine. It is only the world that is different.

Let's have a quick look at the record over a longer stretch. International economic integration – one facet of 'globalization', in a neutral sense of the term – increased rapidly before the First World War, stagnated or declined during the interwar years, and resumed after the Second World War, now reaching levels of a century ago by gross measures; the fine structure is much more complex. By some measures, globalization was greater before the First World War: one illustration is 'free circulation of labour', the foundation of free trade for Adam Smith, though not for his contemporary admirers. By other measures, globalization is far greater now: one dramatic example – not the only one – is the flow of short-term speculative capital, far beyond any precedent. The distinction reflects some central features of the version of globalization preferred by the masters of the universe: to an extent even beyond the norm, capital has priority, people are incidental.

The Mexican border is an interesting example. It is artificial, the result of conquest, like most borders, and has been porous in both directions for a variety of socioeconomic reasons. It was militarized after NAFTA by Clinton,[7] thus erecting barriers to 'free circulation of labour'. That was necessary because of the anticipated effects of NAFTA in Mexico: an 'economic miracle', which would be a disaster for much of the population, who would seek to escape. In the same years, the flow of capital, already very free, was expedited further, along with what is called 'trade', mostly centrally managed within private tyrannies, increasingly so post-NAFTA.[8] That is 'trade' only by doctrinal decision. The effects of NAFTA on trade in some meaningful sense of the term have not been examined, to my knowledge.

A more technical measure of globalization is convergence to a global market, with a single price and wage. That plainly has not happened. With respect to incomes at least, the opposite is more likely true, insofar as the rules of the game have been followed. Though much depends on exactly how it is measured, there is good reason to believe that inequality has increased within and across countries that have kept to the rules. That is expected to continue. US intelligence agencies, with the participation of specialists from the academic professions and the private sector, recently released a report on expectations for 2015.[9] They expect 'globalization' to proceed on course: 'Its evolution will be rocky, marked by chronic financial volatility and a widening economic divide.' That means less convergence, less globalization in the technical sense, but more globalization in the doctrinally preferred sense. Financial volatility implies still slower growth and more crises and poverty.

It is at this point that a clear connection is established between 'globalization' in the sense of the masters of the universe, and the increasing likelihood of war. Military planners adopt the same projections, and have explained, forthrightly, that these expectations lie behind the vast expansion of military power. Even pre-9/11, US military expenditures far surpassed those of any potential combination of adversaries. The terror attacks have been exploited to increase the funding sharply, delighting key elements of the private economy. The most ominous programme is militarization of space, also being expanded under the pretext of 'fighting terror'.

The reasoning behind these programmes is explained publicly in Clinton-era documents. A prime reason is the gap between the 'haves' and the 'have-nots', which planners expect to grow, contrary to economic theory but consistent with reality. The 'have-nots' – the 'great beast' of the world – may become disruptive, and must be controlled, in the interests of what is called 'stability' in technical jargon, meaning in practice subordination to the dictates of the masters. That requires means of violence, and having 'assumed, out of self-interest, responsibility for the welfare of the world capitalist system',[10] the United States must be far in the lead. Overwhelming dominance in conventional forces and weapons of mass destruction is not sufficient. It is necessary to move on to the new frontier: militarization of space, undermining the Outer Space Treaty of 1967, so far observed. Recognizing the intent, the UN General Assembly has reaffirmed the Treaty several times; the United States has refused to join, in virtual isolation. And Washington has blocked negotiations at the UN Conference on Disarmament for the past year over this issue – all scarcely reported, for the usual reasons. It is not wise to allow citizens to know of plans that may bring to an end biology's only experiment with 'higher intelligence'.

As is widely observed, these programmes benefit military industry, but we should bear in mind that the term is misleading. Throughout modern history, but with a dramatic increase after the Second World War, the military system has been used as a device to socialize cost and risk while privatizing profit. The 'new economy' is to a substantial extent an outgrowth of the dynamic and innovative state sector of the US economy. The main reason that public spending in biological sciences has been rapidly increasing is that intelligent right-wingers understand that the cutting edge of the economy is shifting from electronics-based to biology-based, and must continue to rely on these public initiatives. A huge increase is scheduled under the pretext of bioterror, just as the public was deluded into paying for the new economy under the pretext that 'the Russians are coming' or after they collapsed, by the threat of the 'technological sophistication' of Third World countries as the party line shifted in 1990, instantly, without missing a beat and with scarcely a word of comment.[11] That is also a reason that national security exceptions have to be part of international economic agreements: it doesn't help Haiti, but it allows the US economy to grow under the traditional principle of harsh market discipline for the poor and a nanny state for the rich – what's called 'neo-liberalism', though it is not a very good term: the doctrine is centuries old, and would scandalize classical liberals.

One might argue that these public expenditures were often worthwhile. Perhaps, perhaps not. Perhaps if there had been a democratic choice, the population would have preferred to spend public funds for health care, education, decent living and work conditions, sustainable development and a liveable environment for their grandchildren, and other such choices, rather than the glories of the 'new economy'. But it is clear that the masters were unwilling to allow democratic choice. All of this is concealed from the general public, though the participants understand it very well.

Plans to cross the last frontier of violence by militarization of space are sometimes disguised as 'missile defence', but anyone who pays attention to history knows that when we hear the word 'defence', we should think 'offence'. The present case is no exception. The goal is quite frankly stated: to ensure 'global dominance', 'hegemony'. Official documents stress prominently that the goal is 'to protect US interests and investment', and control the 'have-nots'. Today that requires domination of space, just as in earlier times the most powerful states created armies and navies 'to protect and enhance their commercial interests'.[12] It is recognized that these new initiatives, in which the United States is far in the lead, pose a serious threat to survival. And it is also understood that they could be prevented by international treaties. But as I've already mentioned, hegemony is a higher value than survival, a moral calculus that has prevailed among the powerful throughout history. What has changed is that the stakes are much higher, awesomely so.

The relevant point here is that the expected success of 'globalization' in the doctrinal sense is a primary reason given for the programmes of using space for offensive weapons of instant mass destruction.

Let us return to 'globalization', and 'the greatest economic boom in America's history – and the world's' in the 1990s.

Since the Second World War, the international economy has passed through two major phases: the Bretton Woods phase to the early 1970s, and the period since, with the dismantling of the Bretton Woods system of regulated exchange rates and controls on capital movement. It is the second phase that is commonly called 'globalization', associated with the neo-liberal policies of the 'Washington consensus'. The two phases are quite different. The first is often called the 'golden age' of (state) capitalism. The second phase has been accompanied by marked deterioration in standard macroeconomic measures: rate of growth of the economy and capital investment, higher interest rates (harming economies), vast accumulation of unproductive reserves to protect currencies, increased financial volatility, and other harmful consequences.[13] There were exceptions, notably the East Asian countries that did not follow the rules: they did not worship the 'religion' that 'markets know best', as Joseph Stiglitz wrote in a World Bank research publication shortly before he was appointed chief economist, later removed (and winning the Nobel prize).[14] In contrast, the worst results were found where the rules were rigorously applied, as in Latin America, facts widely acknowledged, among others, by José Antonio Ocampo, Executive Secretary of the Economic Commission for Latin America and the Caribbean (ECLAC), in an address before the American Economic Association in 2001.[15] The 'promised land is a mirage', he observed; growth in the 1990s was far below that of the three decades of 'state-led development' in Phase One. He too noted that the correlation between following the rules and poor economic outcomes holds worldwide.

Let us return, then, to the profound and troubling dilemma: the rapid growth and great prosperity brought by globalization have brought inequality because some lack skills. There is no dilemma, because the rapid growth and prosperity are a myth.

Many international economists regard liberalization of capital as a substantial factor in the poorer outcomes of Phase Two.[16] But the economy is a complex affair, so that one has to be cautious about causal connections. One consequence of liberalization of capital, however, is rather clear: it undercuts democracy. That was understood by the framers of Bretton Woods. One reason that the agreements were founded on regulation of capital was to allow governments to carry out social democratic policies, which had enormous popular support. Free capital movement creates what has been called a 'virtual Senate' with 'veto power' over government decisions, sharply restricting policy options. Governments face a 'dual constituency': voters, and speculators, who 'conduct moment-by-moment referendums' on government policies.[17] Even in the rich countries, the private constituency tends to prevail.

Other components of the investor-rights version of 'globalization' have similar consequences. Socioeconomic decisions are increasingly shifted to unaccountable concentrations of power, an essential feature of neo-liberal 'reforms' (a term of propaganda, not description). Extension of the attack on democracy is presumably being planned, without public discussion, in the negotiations for a General Agreement on Trade in Services (GATS). The term 'services' refers to just about anything that might fall within the arena of democratic choice: health, education, welfare, postal and other communications, water and other resources and so on. There is no meaningful sense in which transferring such services to private hands is 'trade', but the term has been so deprived of meaning that it might as well be extended to this travesty as well.

The huge public protests in Quebec in April 2000 at the Summit of the Americas, set in motion by the freaks in Porto Alegre several months earlier, were in part directed against the attempt to impose the GATS principles in secret within the planned Free Trade Area of the Americas (FTAA). Those protests brought together a very broad constituency, North and South, all strongly opposed to what is apparently being planned by trade ministers and corporate executives behind closed doors.

The protests did receive coverage, of the usual kind: the freaks are throwing rocks and disrupting the wizards thinking about the big problems. The invisibility of their actual concerns is quite remarkable. For example, *New York Times* economics correspondent Anthony DePalma writes that the GATS agreement 'has generated none of the public controversy that has swirled around [WTO] attempts to promote merchandise trade', even after Seattle.[18] In fact, it has been a prime concern for years. As in other cases, this is not deceit. DePalma's knowledge about the freaks is presumably based on what passes through the media filter, and it is an iron law of journalism that the serious concerns of activists must be rigidly barred, in favour of someone throwing a rock, perhaps a police provocateur.

The importance of protecting the public from information was revealed dramatically at the April Summit. Every editorial office in the United States had on its desk two important studies, timed for release just before the Summit. One was from Human Rights Watch (HRW), the second from the Economic Policy Institute in Washington; neither organization is exactly obscure.[19] Both studies investigated in depth the effects of NAFTA, which was hailed at the Summit as a grand triumph and a model for the FTAA, with headlines trumpeting its praises by George Bush and other leaders, all accepted as Gospel Truth. Both studies were suppressed in the United States with near-total unanimity. It's easy to see why. HRW analyzed the effects of NAFTA on labour rights, which, it found, were harmed in all three participating countries. The EPI report was more comprehensive: it consisted of detailed analyses of the effects of NAFTA on working people, written by specialists on the three countries. The conclusion is that this is one of the rare agreements that has harmed the majority of the population in all of the participating countries.

The detailed inquiries of the EPI confirm what had been reported in the business press and academic studies. 'By 2000 the real minimum wage had fallen to 50 percent of its 1980 value', Mexico business correspondent Lucy Conger reported, while 'a *Wall Street Journal* poll taken in 1999 found that 43 percent of Mexicans say their parents' standard of living 30 years ago was better than theirs today'.[20] The *Journal* reported further that although the Mexican economy was growing rapidly in the late 1990s, after a sharp post-NAFTA decline, consumers suffered a 40 per cent drop in purchasing power, the number of people living in extreme poverty grew twice as fast as the population, and even those working in foreign-owned assembly plants lost purchasing power. Similar conclusions were drawn in a study of the Latin American section of the Woodrow Wilson Centre, which also found that economic power had greatly concentrated as small Mexican companies cannot obtain financing, traditional farming sheds workers, and labour-intensive sectors (agriculture, light industry) cannot compete internationally with what is called 'free enterprise' in the doctrinal system. Agriculture suffered for the usual reasons: peasant farmers cannot compete with highly subsidized US agribusiness, with effects familiar throughout the world.[21]

Most of this was predicted by critics of NAFTA, including the ignored Office of Technology Assessment (OTA) and labour movement studies. Critics were wrong in one respect, however. Most anticipated a sharp increase in the urban–rural ratio, as hundreds of thousands of peasants were driven off the land. That didn't happen. The reason, it seems, is that conditions deteriorated so badly in the cities that there was a huge flight from them as well to the United States. Those who survive the crossing – many do not – work for very low wages, with no benefits, under awful conditions. The effect is to destroy lives and communities in Mexico and to improve the US economy, where 'consumption of the urban middle class continues to be subsidized by the impoverishment of farm laborers both in the United States and Mexico', the Woodrow Wilson Centre study points out.

These are among the costs of NAFTA, and neo-liberal globalization generally, that economists generally choose not to measure. But even by the highly ideological standard measures, the costs have been severe.

None of this was allowed to sully the celebration of NAFTA and the FTAA at the Summit. Unless they are connected to activist organizations, most people know about these matters only from their own lives. And carefully protected from reality by the free press, many regard themselves as somehow failures, unable to take part in the celebration of the greatest economic boom in history.

Protests at the summit were too visible to ignore, however, and were widely reported, in the usual fashion: anarchists throwing rocks and so on. The summit rhetoric did take some notice of the concerns of the protestors, placing great emphasis not only on the heralded performance of the NAFTA model, but also on democracy and transparency.[22] Its character was described by the *Financial Times*, departing from the celebratory norm in the United States:

> In an effort to show that they were listening to dissenting voices, the Canadian hosts organised a get-together between a group of ministers and representatives of 'civil society'. The event turned out to be a turgid public relations exercise at which a string of exquisitely well-mannered speakers – many of them university academics – trotted out their viewpoints in presentations limited to a maximum of three minutes. But when the organisers spotted that some journalists – who might have asked a few hard-hitting questions – were in the audience, they ejected them.... So much for all those pious ministerial commitments to transparency in global policymaking.[23]

Data from the richest country in the world are enlightening, but I will skip the details.[24] The picture generalizes, with some variation of course, and exceptions of the kind already noted. The picture is much worse when we depart from standard economic measures. One cost is the threat to survival implicit in the reasoning of military planners, already described. There are many others. To take one, the International Labour Organization reported a rising worldwide epidemic of serious mental health disorders, often linked to stress in the workplace, with very substantial fiscal costs in the industrial countries. A large factor, they conclude, is 'globalization', which brings loss of job security, pressure on workers, and a higher workload, particularly in the United States. Is this a cost of 'globalization'? From one point of view, it is one of its most attractive features. When he lauds the performance of the US economy over which he presides, Alan Greenspan often stresses that an important factor in the success is 'atypical restraint on compensation increases [which] appears to be mainly the consequence of greater worker insecurity', which leads to reduced costs for employers. The World Bank agrees. It recognizes that 'labor market flexibility' has acquired 'a bad name ... as a euphemism for pushing wages down and workers out', but nevertheless 'is essential in all the regions of the world.... The most important reforms involve lifting constraints on labor mobility and wage flexibility, as well as breaking the ties between social services and labor contracts.'[25]

In brief, pushing workers out, pushing wages down, undermining benefits are all crucial contributions to economic health, according to prevailing ideology.

Unregulated trade has further benefits for corporations. Much, probably most, 'trade' is centrally managed through a variety of devices: intra-firm transfers, strategic alliances, outsourcing and others. Broad trading areas benefit corporations by making them less answerable to local and national communities. This enhances the effects of neo-liberal programmes, which regularly have reduced labour share of income. In the United States, the 1990s were the first post-war period when division of income shifted strongly to owners of capital, away from labour. Trade has a wide range of unmeasured costs: subsidizing energy, resource depletion, and other externalities not counted. It also brings advantages, though here too some caution is necessary. The most widely hailed is that trade increases specialization – which reduces choices, including the choice to modify comparative advantage, otherwise known as 'development'. Choice and development are values in themselves: undermining them is a substantial cost. If the American colonies had been compelled to accept the WTO regime 200 years ago, New England would be pursuing its comparative advantage in exporting fish, surely not producing textiles, which survived only by exorbitant tariffs to bar British products (mirroring Britain's treatment of India). The same was true of steel and other industries, right to the present, particularly in the highly protectionist Reagan years, which broke post-war records – even putting aside the state sector of the economy. There is a great deal to say about all of this. Much of the story is masked in selective modes of economic measurement, though it is well known to economic historians and historians of technology.

The rules of the game are likely to enhance deleterious effects for the poor. The rules of the WTO bar the mechanisms used by every rich country to reach its current state of development, while also providing unprecedented levels of protectionism for the rich, including a patent regime that bars innovation and growth in novel ways, and allows corporate entities to amass huge profits by monopolistic pricing of products often developed with substantial public contribution.

Under contemporary versions of traditional mechanisms, half the people in the world are effectively in receivership, their economic policies managed by experts in Washington. But even in the rich countries democracy is under attack by virtue of the shift of decision-making power from governments, which may be partially responsive to the public, to private tyrannies, which have no such defects. Cynical slogans such as 'trust the people' or 'minimize the state' do not, under current circumstances, call for increasing popular control. They shift decisions from governments to other hands, but not 'the people': rather, the management of collectivist legal entities, largely unaccountable to the public, and effectively totalitarian in internal structure, much as conservatives charged a century ago when opposing the corporatization of America.

Latin American specialists and polling organizations have observed for some years that the extension of formal democracy in Latin America has been accompanied by increasing disillusionment about democracy, alarming trends, which continue, analysts have observed, noting the link between 'declining economic fortunes' and 'lack of faith' in democratic institutions. As Argentinean political scientist Atilio Boron pointed out some years ago, the new wave of democratization in Latin America coincided with neo-liberal economic 'reforms', which undermine effective democracy, a phenomenon that extends worldwide, in various forms.[26]

To the United States as well. A Harvard University project that monitors political attitudes found that the 'feeling of powerlessness has reached an alarming high', with more than half saying that people like them have little or no influence on what government does, a sharp rise through the neo-liberal period.[27]

Issues on which the public differs from elites (economic, political, intellectual) are pretty much off the agenda, notably questions of economic policy. One would have been hard pressed, for example, to find discussion of the Summit of the Americas and the FTAA, and other topics that involve issues of prime concern for the public. Voters instead are directed to what the PR industry calls 'personal qualities', not 'issues'.

What remains of democracy is to be construed as the right to choose among commodities. Business leaders have long explained the need to impose on the population a 'philosophy of futility' and 'lack of purpose in life', to 'concentrate human attention on the more superficial things that comprise much of fashionable consumption'. Deluged by such propaganda from infancy, people may then accept their meaningless and subordinate lives and forget ridiculous ideas about managing their own affairs. They may abandon their fate to the wizards, and in the political realm, to the self-described 'intelligent minorities' who serve and administer power.

The struggle to impose that regime takes many forms, but never ends, and never will as long as high concentrations of effective decision-making power remain in place. It is only reasonable to expect the masters to exploit any opportunity that comes along – at the moment, the fear and anguish of the population in the face of terrorist attacks, a serious matter for the West now that, with new technologies available, it has lost its virtual monopoly of violence, retaining only a huge preponderance.

But there is no need to accept these rules, and those who are concerned with the fate of the world and its people will surely follow a very different course. The popular struggles against investor rights 'globalization', mostly in the South, have influenced the rhetoric, and to some extent the practices, of the masters of the universe, who are concerned and defensive. These popular movements are unprecedented in scale, in range of constituency, and in international solidarity; the meetings at the WSF are a critically important illustration. The future to a large extent lies in their hands. It is hard to overestimate what is at stake.

NOTES

1   This is an edited version of a talk entitled 'A world without war' given at the World Social Forum in Porto Alegre, Brazil, on 1 February 2002. An earlier version appeared in Otero, Carlos (ed.) (2003) *Radical Priorities*, AK Press, Oakland, Calif.

2   See Chomsky, *Deterring Democracy* (Verso, 1991) on the National Security Strategy report of 1990, the invasion of Panama, and other immediate reactions to the fall of the Berlin Wall, effectively ending the Cold War. See Chomsky, *World Orders Old and New* (Columbia, 1994), chapter 2, on the enthusiastic reaction in the business press to the new weapons made available for use against 'pampered' Western workers with their 'luxurious' lifestyles.

3   De Jonquières, Guy (2001) 'Power elite at Davos may be eclipsed by protesters', *Financial Times*, 24 January.

4   *World Orders Old and New*, chapter 2 (see note 2).

5   Burkins, Glenn (1997) 'Labor fights against fast-track trade measure', *Wall Street Journal*, 16 September.

6   Lewis, A (2001) 'The golden eggs', *New York Times*, 10 March.

7   Nevins, Joseph (2002) *Operation Gatekeeper,* Routledge, New York.

8   Quinlan, Joseph and Chandler, Marc (2001) 'The US trade deficit: a dangerous obsession', *Foreign Affairs*, May–June, report that nearly two-thirds of US imports from Mexico are between multinational firms and affiliates. Pre-NAFTA estimates were about 50 per cent.

9   National Intelligence Council (2000) *Global Trends 2015*, NIC, Washington DC.

10   Diplomatic historian Gerald Haines, also senior historian of the CIA, *The Americanization of Brazil* (Scholarly Resources, 1989), describing US policy after the Second World War.

11   See note 2.

12   US Space Command (1997) *Vision for 2020*, February.

13   See among others Weisbrot, Mark, Naiman, Robert and Kim, Joyce (2003) *The Emperor has No Growth: Declining economic growth rates in the era of globalization*, Center for Economic and Policy Research, Washington DC, September; Felix, David (1998) 'Asia and the crisis of financial globalization', in Baker, Dean, Epstein, Gerald and Pollin, Robert (eds),*Globalization and Progressive Economic Policy*, Cambridge University Press, Cambridge, and other articles in the same volume.

14   Stiglitz, Joseph (1996) *World Bank Research Observer* 11:2, August.
15   Ocampo, Antonio (2001) 'Rethinking the development agenda', American Economic Association annual meeting, January.
16   See among others Eatwell, John and Taylor, Lance (2000) Global Finance at Risk, New Press, New York; Felix (1998) and other articles in Epstein and Pollin (see note 13).
17   Mahon, James (1996) *Mobile Capital and Latin American Development* Pennsylvania State University Press, Philadelphia. Canova, Timothy (1999) 'Banking and financial reform at the crossroads of the neoliberal contagion', *American University International Law Review* 14:6; *Brooklyn Law Review* (1995) 'The transformation of US Banking and Finance', 60:4.
18   DePalma, Anthony (2002) 'WTO pact would set global accounting rules', *New York Times*, 1 March.
19   Human Rights Watch (2001) *Trading Away Rights*, Human Rights Watch, April. Economic Policy Institute (2001) *NAFTA at Seven*, Economic Policy Institute, April.
20   Conger, Lucy (2001) 'Mexico's long march to democracy', *Current History*, February.
21   Millman, Joel (1999) 'Is the Mexican model worth the pain?' *Wall Street Journal*, 8 March, cited by Greenfield, Gerard (2001) 'The toxicity of NAFTA's ruling', *Against the Current*, January/February. Bach, Robert L (undated) *Campaigning for Change: Reinventing NAFTA to Serve Immigrants*, Working Paper Series Number 248, Latin American Program, Woodrow Wilson International Center for Scholars, Washington DC.
22   DePalma, Antony (2001) 'Talks tie trade in the Americas to democracy', *New York Times*, 23 April, p 1.
23   *Financial Times* (2001) 'Breathless at the Summit', 23 April.
24   See the regular biennial studies of the Economic Policy Institute, *The State of Working America.*
25   Greenspan, Alan, testimony before Senate Banking Committee, February 1997, cited by Editorial, *Multinational Monitor*, March 1997. World Bank (1995) *World Development Report 1995: Workers in an integrated world*, Oxford University Press, Oxford, cited by Levinson, Jerome (1999) 'The international financial system: a flawed architecture', *Fletcher Forum*, Winter/Spring.
26   Boron, Atilio (1996) 'Democracy or neoliberalism?' *Boston Review*, October/November; see his *State, Capitalism, and Democracy in Latin America* (Lynne Rienner, Boulder, Colo., 1996).

27 Patterson, Thomas (2000) 'Will Democrats find victory in the ruins?'
    Boston Globe Op-Ed, 15 December; 'Point of agreement: we're glad it's
    over', *New York Times* Op-Ed, 8 November; *The Vanishing Voter*
    (Knopf, 2002), p 126. For more on the elections, see my articles in *Z
    magazine*, January and February 2001.

2 Britain and the G8:
a champion of the world's poor?[1]

Mark Curtis

In 2005, Britain is hosting (or by the time you read this book will have hosted) the summit meeting of the G8 countries in Gleneagles, Scotland. New Labour ministers have been clamouring to publicly demonstrate their commitment to global development issues. But how seriously should we take these public positions?

According to Prime Minister Tony Blair, 'real development can only come through partnership. Not the rich dictating to the poor. Not the poor demanding from the rich. But matching rights and responsibilities.'[2] This is Blair's world – where the poor have no right to make demands on the rich. Yet this is a world where half the population lives in poverty, on an average of US$2 a day, while the richest few dozen individuals command more wealth than hundreds of millions of people. In this situation, are the poor really not entitled to be 'demanding from the rich' rather than simply 'matching rights and responsibilities'?

Blair's view is echoed by Chancellor Gordon Brown, who has outlined a 'global new deal' based on the poorest and richest countries 'each meeting our obligations'. The poorest countries' 'obligations' are 'to pursue stability and create the conditions for new investment'. The richest countries' obligations are 'to open our markets and to transfer resources'.[3] One might think that the world's poorest countries have no obligations to the rich, after centuries of exploitation and enduring extreme poverty partly because of an international economic system that plainly disadvantages them. But no, those with few schools, health services and safe water are deemed by New Labour to have 'obligations' to us concerning helping our companies to make more profits (creating 'the conditions for new investment').

Yet Blair and Brown are regarded throughout the mainstream media and liberal political culture as champions of the world's poor. Their policies on aid, Africa and even trade are routinely widely praised, as demonstrating that, more recently, even though they might be liars and criminals over Iraq, on global development they are committed internationalists. It is an extraordinary view. Because, putting the progressive rhetoric aside, government ministers have also made plain their other goals – which are more plausible and confirmed by their actual policies. This is easy to spot, if we bother to look.

THE NEW LIBERALIZATION THEOLOGISTS

The basic fact is that Britain under New Labour is one of the world's leading champions of the neo-liberal economic model that is essentially being imposed on the much of the rest of the world, and which is generally increasing poverty and inequality. Britain's basic priority – which I have tried to document in recent books[4] – is to aid British companies in getting their hands on other countries' resources. The explicit goal is to break into foreign markets. Trade Secretary Patricia Hewitt has said that 'we want to open up protected markets in developing countries'. A new World Trade Organization (WTO) round of negotiations 'is the best way of ensuring that our businesses can benefit from, and contribute to, future economic growth anywhere in the world', she stated in July 2001.[5]

'Opening up markets and cutting duties around the world' will 'create new opportunities for our service sectors', Hewitt adds. Similarly, Trade Minister Baroness Symons assured a big business lobby group on services that the government was committed 'to work with you to bring those [trade] barriers down'. She said that 'there is still a lot to be done in India – and other markets – to facilitate market access for industry'.[6]

Former Trade Secretary Margaret Beckett wrote in the *Financial Times* that a key objective of the Department of Trade and Industry is:

> to continue developing the conditions, at home and abroad, in which British business can thrive.... Britain's businesses need to be able to trade throughout the world's markets as easily as they can in home markets without facing high tariffs, discriminatory regulations or unnecessarily burdensome procedures.[7]

Essentially the same goal was repeated in the government's White Paper on trade produced in July 2004:

> The UK government has a key role to play at the international policy level to ensure that any distortions created by other government interventions are minimised so that the UK can compete in global markets, while deriving the maximum benefit from competition from increased imports.[8]

Securing businesses' access into foreign markets is the aim of economic 'liberalization'. Under New Labour, Britain has been perhaps the world's leading champion of trade liberalization, which it wants to see applied in all countries. Policies like import tariffs and subsidies, raised by governments to protect their markets from competition that can undermine domestic industry or agriculture, are seen as essentially heretical for developing countries ('trade-distorting', in the theology). 'Trade liberalization is the only sure route' to economic growth and prosperity for developing countries, Tony Blair says with religious conviction.[9]

The rich North's aim is to 'lock in' all countries to this agenda, while the WTO has become in effect an organizing body for the global economy. Peter Sutherland, former Director-General of the WTO, for example, has said that an aim of the trade negotiations was to extend liberalization 'to most aspects of domestic policy-making' affecting international trade and investment. The promotion of this one-size-fits-all economic ideology mainly benefits transnational corporations (TNCs). As the Chief Trade Economist of the World Bank has said, 'The dynamic behind the WTO process has been the export interests of major enterprises in the advanced trading countries.' The purpose of global trade policy, explained Lawrence Summers, a former World Bank chief economist and Clinton administration official, is to 'ensure viable investment opportunities for OECD companies'.[10]

If a prize were to be given for exploiting 9/11 for one's own ends, then Trade Secretary Patricia Hewitt would surely be one of the front runners. An aide to Transport Secretary Stephen Byers suggested in an internal memo that the government take advantage of 9/11 to push through some unpopular policies; the aide and Byers were hounded by the media for weeks, contributing to Byers's eventual resignation. By contrast, Hewitt said something worse openly – that the attack on the World Trade Centre 'was also an attack on global trade'. 'So we must respond by launching a new trade round' and 'fight terror with trade' in the upcoming WTO negotiations, which were then two months away.[11] Thus the dead of 9/11 were being used to push further 'liberalization' on the world's poor.

At that WTO summit in Qatar, the British government led the way in pushing for a new trade round that would have added new issues – such as investment and procurement – to the WTO's negotiating remit. This was opposed by developing countries, which by adopting a united stance just managed to prevent the rich countries securing this goal. Two years later, Britain and the European Union continued to push these new issues in the run-up to the Cancun ministerial meeting in late 2003 – developing countries again remained united and eventually forced the European Union to back down.

A key British aim in the WTO has been to secure a global agreement on investment that would require all governments to give 'equal treatment' to foreign and domestic businesses in many important economic policy areas. This would be a disaster for many developing countries: all successful developers in the past have strongly discriminated in favour of their domestic companies, nurturing them to become competitive, to aid national development. If foreign companies are treated equally, an important development policy is removed and local markets can be dominated by foreign enterprises. In turn, profits can simply be repatriated to the home country and poor countries drained of scarce resources.

Britain has been pushing for 'treating inward investors exactly the same as domestic investors – ownership of the company should not be relevant to the application of national laws and regulations'. The aim of a global agreement, Baroness Symons explains, is to 'help lock in individual countries' own investment reform efforts' – that is, ensure they promote the one-size-fits-all model.[12]

Britain was one of the strongest supporters of the proposed Multilateral Agreement on Investment (MAI) that Northern countries tried to negotiate in the OECD, but which was eventually scuppered in 1998, partly due to an NGO campaign against it. If passed into law, the MAI would have massively increased the power of corporations over elected governments, greatly expanding their investment rights all over the world. After the talks collapsed, the British government immediately said that 'it is better to start afresh in another forum' than the OECD, given its 'long-standing objective' of pursuing investment negotiations in the WTO.[13]

Asked by a parliamentary committee whether an international investment agreement was needed, then Trade Minister Brian Wilson replied that, 'As to whether there is a demand from UK companies for some such agreement, I can assure you that this is a subject that is raised with us very regularly by UK companies which invest abroad.'[14]

The government has also consistently acted as an ally to big business in the ongoing WTO negotiations on services. Trade Minister Baroness Symons has told members of International Finance Services London – a big-business pressure group – that Whitehall is seeking 'an international trading environment in which UK business can compete and thrive'. She added: 'I hope you will view this government as your greatest ally in moving that agenda forward', including through the WTO. After the Qatar ministerial, Symons said that the WTO negotiations 'offer a huge opportunity to European and British businesses'. In services, 'we need to continue to ensure that the UK's key offensive interests are reflected.'[15]

Services are big business to Britain, which is the second largest exporter of services in the world, amounting to £67 billion in 2000, and the fourth largest importer. Symons notes that for Britain, 'trading services internationally is of far greater importance than it is to a number of countries', which explains why to New Labour's liberalization theologists, 'open markets are a major economic interest and essential to our own economic performance'.[16]

THE IMPORTANCE OF DFID

New Labour created a new instrument for promoting these interests – the Department for International Development (DFID). Under the present government an extremist economic project is being pursued under a great moral pretext – that global 'liberalization' will promote development and the eradication of poverty. A variety of initiatives have been established, and numerous ministerial speeches made, to reassure business of the benefits of New Labour's policies, emphasizing that business is a 'partner' in development. Indeed, DFID has not hidden the fact that it acts as a high-level global lobbyist for big business. Consider then International Development Secretary Clare Short's speech to business leaders at Lancaster House in April 1999:

> The assumption that our moral duties and business interests are in conflict is now demonstrably false....
> I am very keen that we maximise the impact of our shared interest in business and development by working together in partnership.... We bring access to other governments and influence in the multilateral system – such as the World Bank and IMF.... You are well aware of the constraints business faces in the regulatory environment for investment in any country.... Your ideas on overcoming these constraints can be invaluable when we develop our country strategies. We can use this understanding to inform our dialogue

with governments and the multilateral institutions on the reform agenda.[17]

So DFID is offering itself as an instrument for business to shape the policies of multilateral institutions and developing country governments. This is at least an honest admission, and has been the subject of various other speeches by DFID and Department of Trade and Industry ministers.

DFID policy is to help minimize the risks for private investors in developing countries and 'to develop an investor friendly environment' and 'a more favourable business environment'. Its Business Partnership Unit is a first point of contact for business and looks at 'ways in which DFID can improve the enabling environment for productive investment overseas and how we can contribute to the operation of the overseas financial sector'. DFID is also working with the World Bank's Business Partners for Development programme, involving governments, businesses and some NGOs in the water, transport and extractive industries sectors. Its bilateral aid programmes 'provide governments of developing countries with the advice and expertise to help attract private finance'. It also supports the World Bank's Private–Public Infrastructure Advisory Facility, which provides 'advice' on regulatory frameworks to attract foreign investment.[18]

Domestically and internationally, the government is actively campaigning for the minimum regulation of business. Clare Short said that 'By far the best approach is for enterprises themselves to ensure that they respect the rights of workers, protect their health and safety and offer satisfactory conditions of employment.... Voluntary codes ... are often more effective than regulation.'[19]

It might be thought astonishing that a Labour leader believes that businesses should be left to themselves to ensure they respect the rights of workers! But not if the strategy is to act as a great protector of transnational business. New Labour's consistent rejection of proposals for legally binding regulation of corporations to protect people contrasts starkly with its vociferous support for legally binding WTO rules that benefit business. An obvious agenda for any British government concerned with promoting a positive development agenda would be to rein in the worst aspects of TNC activities. Labour has chosen the opposite route – working to empower TNCs and actively lobbying in their favour. I can find no statement where the government has even seriously criticized TNCs for the harmful effects they can have on the world's poor.

Under New Labour the aid programme has been overtly used to push corporate globalization, as the World Development Movement (WDM) is increasingly uncovering. Christian Aid found that in Ghana, the British government was in effect tying the release of British aid to Ghana's government privatizing water services. DFID was withholding £10 million in aid for the expansion of water supply in the city of Kumasi until company bids for the leases of Ghana's urban water supplies had been received. DFID had commissioned the Adam Smith Institute – a wholesale advocate of privatization – to 'advise' the British government on restructuring the water sector in Ghana. British water and construction companies have been waiting in the wings to take advantage of privatization.[20]

A recent War on Want report reveals that the government has provided over £100 million of taxpayers' aid money to consultancies such as the Adam Smith Institute, Halcrow and KPMG to push privatization.[21] The government is pressing for the privatization of water supplies and other services across the planet. DFID's chief civil servant notes that 'we are ... extending our support for privatisation in the poorest countries from the power sector in India to the tea industry in Nepal'.[22]

[52]

The difference between developing countries choosing and being forced to accept the Northern countries' agenda is often wafer thin. A number of levers are used by Northern countries to secure their goals. Indeed, even though the WTO agreement does not formally require developing countries to liberalize their services sectors, for example, this is in practice happening thanks to pressure outside the WTO, as in Ghana. As Baroness Symons explains, privatization 'is a growing phenomenon worldwide.... This is occurring quite independently of the GATS negotiations.'[23]

GOVERNMENT ARGUMENTS

What of the government's arguments that it is pursuing a positive development agenda? First, it should be said that this case can only be made by ignoring the wealth of evidence concerning the very clear strategy of promoting corporate globalization and the empowerment of business outlined above. Yet three cases in particular are still routinely made: on trade, aid and debt.

On trade, the government's slogan is that it is promoting 'free and fair trade' – a conflation of two generally conflicting policies that, one might think, would generally be ridiculed. Not so, however; the government receives widespread praise, in some NGO circles as well as the mainstream media, for championing the cause of opening up EU markets to developing countries by removing trade barriers. Certainly, the European Union's blocking such market access at the same time as forcing open developing country markets is gross hypocrisy, and the British government has been outspoken on this. But the reality is that the government sees market access for developing countries as a sweetener for poor countries to do likewise. According to former Trade Minister Richard Caborn, access to

EU markets 'is the message we need to hammer home if we are to get the developing world to agree to another round of WTO talks', that is, further liberalization.[24] It is a myth that mutual liberalization creates a level playing field from which all countries will benefit equally; rather, it is mainly TNCs who gain, poised as they are to take advantage of newly opened markets.

A second area where the government is often praised is in increasing overseas aid. New Labour has increased the aid budget significantly, from a low point at the end of Conservative rule. But, as noted above, aid is routinely used to press developing country governments into promoting neo-liberal economic policies, which can completely undermine the positive impact that better aid could have. For example, Gordon Brown's widely praised flagship aid initiative – the International Finance Facility (IFF) – is billed by the government as doubling overseas aid. WDM's analysis is that the IFF will actually result in less aid over the long term; moreover, such aid remains conditional on developing countries 'opening up to trade and investment'. The government has abolished formal tied aid – aid given on the specific condition that it is used to buy goods from the donor – but the use of such 'globalized aid' has been increasing.

The same goes for debt relief. In this area, Britain has a more positive record than other G8 governments. It was largely public pressure – notably through the Jubilee 2000 debt campaign – that pushed the government into its more progressive stance. Yet debt relief is also only provided on condition that countries implement World Bank/IMF programmes that require policies of economic liberalization – in effect, a reward for developing countries promoting policies that will further impoverish them, perhaps a bit like a doctor offering a patient an aspirin at the same time as injecting them with a deadly disease. The fact that debt relief is such a lever over developing countries – a tool in the armoury of promoting corporate globalization – plausibly offers one explanation why New Labour has become keen on it.

In this context, the task of campaigners is to ensure that government rhetoric is exposed and that the public sees accurately what policies are being promoted in their name. In the short term, a more effective campaigning challenge needs to be mounted to government policies; in the long term, efforts need to be stepped up to enhance the global justice movement to reverse corporate globalization and promote just alternatives.

NOTES

1   This article is an updated extract from *Web of Deceit: Britain's real role in the world*, Vintage, London, 2003, chapter 9.

2   Speech by Tony Blair, Cape Town, 8 January 1999, <www.dfid.gov.uk>.

3   Speech by Gordon Brown, New York, 16 November 2001, <www.hmtreasury.gov.uk>.

4   See *Web of Deceit* (note 1) and *Unpeople: Britain's secret human rights abuses*, Vintage, London, 2004.

5   Speech by Patricia Hewitt, Washington, 24 July 2001, <www.dti.gov.uk>.

6   Speech by Baroness Symons, London, 13 February 2002, <www.fco.gov.uk>; 'Hewitt welcomes breakthrough for world trade landmark agreement at Doha summit', undated, <www.dti.gov.uk>.

7   Beckett, Margaret (1997) 'Towards full market access', *Financial Times*, 10 July.

8   Secretary of State for Trade and Industry (2004) *Trade and Investment White Paper 2004: Making globalisation a force for good*, July, Cm6278, p 61.

9   Speech by Tony Blair, Davos, 18 January 2000, <www.pm.gov.uk>.

10 Cited in Dunkley, Graham (2000) *The Free Trade Adventure: The WTO, the Uruguay Round and globalism*, Zed, London, p 232; Finger, J Michael and Schuler, Philip (1999) 'Implementation of Uruguay Round commitments: The development challenge', World Bank, mimeo, July.

11 Speech by Patricia Hewitt, London, 6 November 2001, <www.dti.gov.uk>.
12 Speech by George Foulkes, Paris, 20 September 1999, <www.dfid.gov.uk>; Speech by Baroness Symons, 13 May 2002, <www.dti.gov.uk>.
13 House of Commons, *Hansard*, 17 November 1998, col 530.
14 Select Committee on Trade and Industry (1999) *Third Report, Session 1998/99*, para 126 <www.publications.parliament.uk/pa/cm199898>.
15 Speech by Baroness Symons, London, 13 February 2002, <www.fco.gov.uk>.
16 Speech by Baroness Symons, 24 April 2002, <www.fco.gov.uk>.
17 Speech by Clare Short, London, 20 April 1999, <www.dfid.gov.uk>.
18 See *Web of Deceit* (see note 1), p 470, note 14 for sources.
19 Speech by Clare Short, 30 May 2000, <www.dfid.gov.uk>.
20 Christian Aid (2001) *Master or Servant?* Christian Aid, London.
21 War on Want (2004) *Profiting from Poverty*, War on Want, London.
22 Speech by John Vereker, 9 December 1997, <www.dfid.gov.uk>.
23 Speech by Baroness Symons, 24 April 2002, <www.fco.gov.uk>.
24 Speech by Richard Caborn, 7 March 2001, <www.dti.gov.uk>.

3 Democracy

Colin Leys

> While the rulers of the world cloister themselves
> behind the fences of Seattle or Genoa, or ascend into
> the inaccessible eyries of Doha or Kananaskis [or
> Gleneagles]… they leave the rest of the world shut out
> of their deliberations. We are left to shout abuse.…
> They reduce us, in other words, to the mob, and then
> revile the thing they have created.… They, the tiniest
> and most unrepresentative of the world's minorities,
> assert a popular mandate they do not possess, then
> accuse us of illegitimacy. Their rule, unauthorised and
> untested, is sovereign.
>
> George Monbiot, *The Age of Consent*, p 84

The two most obvious characteristics of the G8 are that they are at the heart of the nearest thing we have to a world government, and that they are completely undemocratic. The group was first convened by President Nixon in 1973 to deal with the world-wide financial instability resulting from his own abandonment of dollar convertibility, in the context of an oil crisis and what corporate leaders and their advisers saw as a growing and general 'crisis of governability'. It began as meetings of the finance ministers, and later the four presidents or prime ministers, of the United States, West Germany, France and the United Kingdom. It became the Group of Six, or G6, in 1975 when

Japan and Italy were invited to join, the G7 in 1976 when the United States insisted that Canada be included, and the G8 when post-soviet Russia was formally added in 1998 (although the G7 ministers continue to meet without Russia, which is seen as too weak to merit 100 per cent membership).

No international law or agreement authorizes the members of the G8 to make decisions for the world. No democratically elected international or national assembly has given them any mandate. They are self-appointed and accountable to no one. Yet G8 'summits' are clearly a key element in the process of global policy-making. As the presidents and prime ministers of its member countries change, the G8 is where they are socialized into the dominant economic and political discourse. If a 'Washington consensus' exists, to be implemented by the International Monetary Fund (IMF), the World Bank, the World Trade Organization (WTO), the Bank for International Settlements, the Organisation for Economic Co-operation and Development and so on, the G8 is a key forum for arriving at it. And over the 25 years of its existence these policies have produced unprecedented global inequality, an impending global environmental crisis of barely imaginable proportions, and the prospect of unending 'asymmetric warfare' – the latest euphemism for oppression by military superpowers of popular movements using small arms and fanatics relying on terrorism – as well as endless other wars provoked, at bottom, by conditions of intolerable scarcity.

The undemocratic character of the G8 is mirrored in the IMF and other international agencies through which its policies are implemented, although these have formal constitutions established by international agreements and treaties. The UN Security Council is controlled by the veto power of its permanent members, the IMF and the World Bank are controlled through a US veto, the WTO is controlled through the threat – sometimes implemented – of US economic blackmail, and so on. As Monbiot remarks, 'in terms of accountability, transparency and the ability of their subject peoples to dislodge them by peaceful means, [the IMF etc] are about as democratic as the government of Burma' – even though they constantly preach democracy, transparency and accountability to countries whose economies they effectively control.[1]

But it would be a mistake to think that the undemocratic nature of these global institutions makes them entirely different from the governments of the so-called 'free market democracies'. It would be truer to say that the undemocratic nature of the G8 really reflects the undemocratic nature of the structures below it, from the IMF and the WTO, through regional organizations like the European Union and the Free Trade Area of the Americas, right on down the hierarchy, including the national governments of the members of the G8 themselves. Because the liberal democracy that was widely consolidated prior to the 1970s – chiefly in Western Europe, North America and Australasia – has itself also been hollowed out to the point where little is left but the name.

People know this. In the United States only around half of all eligible voters vote, and in the United Kingdom, which has gone farther and faster than any other country in adopting US-style economic policies, voter turnout has slumped dramatically. In other western European countries it has declined more gradually, but growing public apathy and cynicism about national politics and politicians have been recorded everywhere. Politicians in general are now seen as a caste apart, as 'suits', careerists, rather than as genuine representatives of public opinion or the public interest.

Party membership has plummeted too. Elections are now fought in the media, not on doorsteps, and for this parties need wealthy donors more than rank and file members. And because they can't always control the media, political leaders have increasingly moved to control their own followers. Ministers are kept 'on message' by professional spin doctors. In the United States presidential campaign meetings are carefully confined to the party faithful, so that television cameras record only wild enthusiasm. In Europe party conferences are no longer, if they ever were, forums for policy debate, but as far as possible platforms on which the leadership can 'unveil' modest policies, devised by ministers' political advisers or corporate-funded 'think-tanks', that they hope will appeal to this or that section of the electoral 'middle ground' within the limits of what is acceptable to the markets. How did all this come about?

We shouldn't exaggerate the degree of genuine democracy that existed, even in Western Europe or North America, in the post-Second World War era. Few MPs or Congressmen came from the same social background as the majority of voters, rich donors had easy access to ministers, well-funded lobbyists ensured that policies unacceptable to powerful interests were watered down or discarded, and the press was overwhelmingly on the side of business. None the less, in the post-war years people voted in large numbers, and their votes were reinforced by the strength of trade unions to which a majority of the work-force belonged – not always highly democratic bodies them-selves, but organized from below and ultimately answerable to their members. Successive governments were obliged to adopt relatively progressive tax policies and provide extensive social security and social insurance against illness (even, though only partially, in the United States) – and, in Europe, a significant degree of public ownership of the economy. For some 25 years there was a limited balance of power.

But by the late 1970s, soon after Nixon unilaterally ended dollar convertibility, the 'New Right' had come to power and secured the abolition of cross-border capital controls, first in Britain and the United States and then, inevitably, almost everywhere else. From then on, if the owners of capital didn't like the policies of any government they could threaten to move their funds elsewhere, driving up the interest rate that the government had to pay to keep them there, and so critically limiting its economic options. Once national governments accepted this new regime, rather than allying themselves against it, they found they had to compete with each other to attract capital by meeting the wishes of capital owners, as registered in the reactions of the financial markets to any new policy announcement or budget item. Power shifted steadily away from voters and unions to shareholders and bondholders. A new era of what the American political scientist Philip Green calls 'pseudo-democracy' had begun.[2]

Under pseudo-democracy elections continue to be held but no one thinks that they make a big difference to what happens afterwards: whatever government is in office, its social and economic policies will be those broadly required by 'the market'. And the major transnational corporations go 'country shopping' to see which government will give them the best deal – the lowest corporate taxes and social security contributions, the cheapest public infrastructure, the toughest trade union laws, the weakest health and safety regulations. Many of them employ more and better-paid lawyers and PR staff than any government department, and they also induce senior civil servants with the offer of huge salaries to change sides and put their inside knowledge of government at the disposal of the corporation instead. As a result their influence on almost every field of policy – whether keeping down the level of the minimum wage or keeping up the price of pharmaceutical drugs, permitting the patenting of genes or approving the sale of hormone-injected beef, blocking regulation of the out-of-town shopping malls that destroy town centres or drilling for oil in wildlife refuges – is seldom successfully counterbalanced by the influence of consumers or citizens. The American *Sierra* magazine lists 300 'crimes' against the environment committed by President George W Bush in his first three and a half years in office, from eviscerating the Environmental Protection Agency to rejecting the Kyoto protocols.[3] Behind every one of these actions – most of them, when revealed to the public, deeply unpopular – lies a story of corporate lobbying and political donations to promote corporate interests.

It may be objected that the Bush administration is exceptional in this respect – exceptionally linked and financially beholden to the energy industry, and exceptionally blatant in its responsiveness to corporate wishes. This may be so. But the dropping from the British cabinet of Michael Meacher, the one senior British politician with a serious interest in environmental issues and some commitment to tackle them, reminds us that the Blair government's record on the environment has been signally weak too.

The story is no different in any other field of policy. The electoral problem confronting Gerhard Schroeder in Germany is instructive. Responding to global pressures to reduce the 'burden' on German businesses, he cuts back on pensions and social security. The Social Democrats' vote collapses in the Länder elections as ordinary people express their anger at the resulting fall in their living standards. Some of their votes go to more progressive parties, but many go to the Greens, who no longer oppose neo-liberalism, or to far-right parties or the Christian Democrats. Schroeder must then follow Blair and Brown in telling his supporters they must choose between his version of neo-liberalism, or the even harsher version that the Christian Democrats will certainly pursue if they are returned to power. Mrs Thatcher's notorious slogan, 'There is no alternative', is thus adopted by social democrats, even if sometimes half-heartedly disguised in the wishful thinking of the 'third way'. The truth is that these former social democrats no longer see any alternative to accepting what New Labour calls the 'new reality' of the power of global market forces. Reluctantly or not, they too become pseudo-democrats.

It is important to stress that the new era of pseudo-democracy is not just a matter of governments trimming their day-to-day policies to suit the interests of globally mobile capital. It involves deep and permanent changes in nation states which ensure that the previous era of more qualified pseudo-democracy will never return. Central banks are made independent, so that monetary policy remains responsive only to the financial markets, not elected politicians. Central government departments are reorganized on business lines and put at the service of business. Public services are 'marketized', partly by handing over more and more tax-funded services to be delivered by private companies at a large and secure profit, and partly by turning public services into 'internal markets', so that every public servant must think like a businessman or woman. Cooperatives, building societies and other forms of popular and collective ownership – even some trade unions – are transformed into market-oriented businesses.

In Britain, for example, university departments seeking to create new posts must come up with 'business plans' showing how the number of students each post will attract will bring in enough funds to pay for the salary. The idea of a new post being created in a field, however intellectually exciting, that has no certain student appeal, is a thing of the past. The governing principle of university development – or hospital development, and the like – is thus no longer intellectual or professional but commercial. (The principle only applies, however, if it does not offend the rich. For example, although tax avoidance – non-payment of taxes by the ingenious exploitation of tax loopholes – is estimated to cost the British government between £25 and

£75 billion a year, even the lower figure being roughly equal to the entire estimated public sector deficit for 2004–5, and the upper one roughly equal to the cost of the entire health service – the government did not propose to increase the number of civil servants employed in tax collection, but to cut their number by 40,500.)[4]

As the new, enhanced kind of pseudo-democracy deepens and consolidates itself in one country after another, the policies it produces further erode the social and cultural bases of such democracy as existed in the post-Second World War years. In the industrialized countries inequalities of income and wealth become more extreme, everyday life is increasingly commercialized, consumerism becomes more all-pervasive, individualism is celebrated and the social solidarities of neighbourhood and church, workplace and class, which underpinned the vote in the post-war years, and made politicians respect the electorate, disappear. Professional politicians increasingly look upon elections as exercises in selling – above all selling images – to electorates that they increasingly see as rather gullible consumer markets, not bodies of people to be mobilized around coherent programmes for social improvement. To win elections they promise to cut taxes further, curb crime and immigration (pandering to xenophobic responses to declining job security), and give people more 'choice' in public services, supposedly to match the choice they have in the supermarkets – even though what people say they want from public services like health and schools is not choice but a reliable high standard everywhere, as with postal services, trains or electricity. Democracy is degraded to a mere game of winning elections while minimizing as far as possible any genuine accountability of politicians to the people.

And this is the best kind of democracy that results from the G8's policies throughout the world. In much of the world the democratic veneer acceptable to the G8 is so thin as to be practically invisible. This is particularly clear in the case of the United States, the dominant member of the G8. Successive US governments, while presenting themselves as champions of democracy, have in practice always preferred amenable dictators (Marcos, Duvalier, Mobutu, Suharto and so on) to democratic governments that are unwilling to support US policies. The attack on Iraq made this very explicit, as Noam Chomsky has consistently pointed out. When the French and German governments declined to join in the attack they were bitterly condemned by the United States, even though their decisions reflected a strong majority of public opinion in their countries; while the British and Spanish governments, which sent troops in spite of even stronger public opposition at home, were praised. Nor was it ever likely that the United States would tolerate the election by Iraqis of a government opposed to the United States and its policies in the Middle East. As the National Security Adviser to the first President Bush said, 'What's going to happen the first time we hold an election in Iraq and it turns out the radicals win? What do you do? We're surely not going to let them take over.'[5]

The undemocratic nature of the G8 thus reflects the pseudo-democratic nature of the Western governments included in it – to say nothing of the highly questionable democratic credentials of Putin's Russia (and the complete lack of them in the case of China, now awarded G8 'observer' status). It especially reflects, of course, US pseudo-democracy – based as it is on the crude gerrymandering of constituency boundaries, political manipulation of voter rolls, the massive electoral influence of big money, uncritical media and very low turnouts – and the anti-democratic attitudes of the kind of US administrations that come to power on this basis.

The G8's undemocratic nature also reflects the fact that it is also a part of another structure of power – the structure of American imperialism. In official circles it is considered impolite to mention this, but the nature of this real but unmentionable structure has actually been made clear by the second Bush administration, with its commitment to realizing the 'Project for the New American Century', with at least 700 military bases around the world, and determined to achieve 'full spectrum (military) dominance', plus comprehensive American surveillance of all the world's communications and American control of space for military purposes. The US empire, however, is not purely or even primarily military, but involves trying to ensure that all international and national development, from energy supplies to trade relations and culture, conforms to US interests, which involves trying to manage and control all the relevant international and supranational political institutions, and to influence effectively all important national states.[6] Looked at from this angle, it is more accurate to see the G8 as a useful element in the US imperium than as part of any emerging structure of global democracy.

Moreover the free-market policies that the G8 are imposing on the rest of the world, especially the impoverished South, are making it less and less likely that even a minimal degree of pseudo-democracy will be established there. In much of sub-Saharan Africa, for example, the chances are surely negligible that even pseudo-democracy can be established in the conditions of social and economic breakdown that G8-sanctioned structural adjustment policies have created. In those conditions power gravitates to whoever has more money and weapons. Even in India, which is always cited as proof that extreme poverty need not be incompatible with democracy, the convergence of the G8's neo-liberal economic policies and right-wing Hindu fundamentalism have put the future of democracy in question. If the recently re-elected Congress government fails to respond effectively to the nationwide reaction against the liberalizing policies of the previous Bharatiya Janata Party (BJP) government, as seems only too likely, the conditions that have sustained fair elections and peaceful transfers of power up to now could swiftly unravel.[7]

To sum up: the G8 is not a champion of democracy, but an emblem of pseudo-democracy. The neo-liberal free-market policies imposed on the world with its approval don't promote democracy. They reduce it to a sham and, frequently, make even the pretence of it impossible.

NOTES

1   Monbiot, George (2003) *The Age of Consent: A manifesto for a new world order*, Harper Perennial, London, pp 152–3.

2   Green, Philip (1985) *Retrieving Democracy: In search of civic equality*, Rowman and Allanheld, New York; and (1998) *Equality and Democracy*, New Press, New York. Samir Amin calls it 'low intensity democracy' and Perry Anderson, 'thin democracy'.

3   See Natural Resources Defense Council (2004) 'The Bush record: more than 300 crimes against nature', *Sierra*, September/October <http://www.sierraclub.org/sierra>.

4   Monbiot, George (2004) 'Publish and be damned', *Guardian*, 28 September.

5   Brent Scowcroft, quoted in Chomsky, Noam (2003) 'Truths and myths about the invasion of Iraq', in Leo Panitch and Colin Leys (eds), *The New Imperial Challenge: Socialist Register 2004*, Merlin Press, London.

6   See Ahmad, Aijaz, 'Imperialism of our time'; Panitch, Leo and Gindin, Sam, 'Global capitalism and American empire'; and Rogers, Paul, 'The US military posture: "a uniquely benign imperialism?"', also in Panitch and Leys (2003) (see note 5).

7   See Desai, Radhika (2004) 'Forward march of Hindutva halted?', *New Left Review*, Nov–Dec.

4 War

Lindsey German

When you say 'capital' you say 'war'. Wars existed of course before capitalism, but it is only under this economic system that they have reached such levels of technological sophistication, such connections with industrialization that they raise the spectre of human annihilation. There was much that was bloody and terrible about the ancient Greek wars or the medieval battles and sieges, but the Trojan horse or the crossbow could not be weapons of mass destruction in the way that nuclear weapons, chemical warfare and carpet bombing now threaten great swathes of humanity.

The history of the twentieth century shows us this. The period from 1914 to 1945 can be seen as a new Thirty Years' War, sandwiched at either end by two world wars and containing within the 'peace' major wars in Spain, China and Ethiopia, as well as imperialist expansion in Europe itself. In living memory millions had faced death, injury and destruction. As capitalism expanded, and became an international system, so its industrial might was harnessed to develop ever bigger and better weapons to enable every individual nation state or empire to compete in death and destruction with all its rivals. The First World War followed a period of intense internationalization of capital, with the Scramble for Africa which established the colonies in Africa and increased competition between the major European powers.

Industrial production and the war drive went hand in hand, with some of the biggest capitalists being the arms manufacturers. The most sophisticated production techniques were harnessed to war production, most hideously when the German multinationals such as IG Farben were involved in the Holocaust when six million Jews died.

There was a strong sense in 1945 that the peoples of the world wanted peace and that they should join together to resolve differences peacefully rather than go to war. There should be cooperation rather than militarism. But this aspiration never reflected the reality. There were many wars in the second half of the twentieth century, including two major combats directly involving the United States in Korea and Vietnam. But the two superpowers' (the United States's and the Soviet Union's) possession of nuclear weapons did to a certain extent produce a 'balance of terror' – the threat of a war using weapons so terrible that they threatened human extinction.

The past 15 years have changed the nature of wars again. There were more wars in the 1990s than at any time since 1945. The major capitalist powers have been centrally involved in many of those wars: in the Gulf War against Iraq in 1991, in the series of Balkan wars following the break-up of Yugoslavia which culminated in the major war against Serbia in 1999, and in the 'war on terror' first against Afghanistan in 2001 and then against Iraq in 2003/4. War, not just the threat of it but its awful and terrible reality, has become a central political feature of countries that had thought they would never see such things again. The main casualties of war are civilians. During the First World War, around 15 per cent of casualties were civilians, while 85 per cent were from the military. In recent wars, the proportion has been the other way round, with civilians often deliberately targeted by belligerent powers.

The changes happened for a number of reasons. The US defeat in Vietnam in the mid-1970s, and its inability to intervene in other countries following that defeat, began to be overcome. US military confidence was greatly increased when the second superpower, the Soviet Union, collapsed and broke up after 40 years in the late 1980s.

The greatest impetus behind the changes, however, was the change in the world economy that has taken place in the past two decades: the huge increase in international financial transactions, the growth of international trade and manufacturing. This meant opening up economies previously closed to the Western powers, and it meant deregulating economies in order to allow the free market to reign. But while global capitalism wanted to open up markets in order to extend its economic might, this brought Western capital into conflict with the populations of many parts of the world. They saw their livelihoods and sometimes even their lives threatened by this deregulation, which threatened traditional industries or farming and looked likely to turn resources that had once been treated as belonging to everyone into expensive commodities. They therefore needed military might as a last resort to help open up these economies, and to stifle or repress local opposition, including sometimes rulers of 'rogue states' who would not acquiesce to their aims.

This war drive has been strengthened by an urge among the world's great powers to intervene strategically in areas previously closed to them. The wars of the past 15 years have been in parts of the world that were not within the Western sphere of influence, such as the Balkans, and with regimes which have operated against the interests of the West. This was true in both Afghanistan and Iraq, where forces once encouraged by the United States have now become its bitterest enemies. The Middle East holds a special economic prize as well: it is the source of much of the world's oil resources, a fact that has led the Western powers to intervene repeatedly to prop up dictatorial regimes and autocratic monarchies in order to ensure a steady flow of this oil. Iraq has over 10 per cent of the world's proven oil supplies, and before the war US multinationals were unable to get their hands on it. Indeed they were threatened by the deals done between Iraq and Russia. War in Iraq provided to them the prospect of political and economic control of this major resource.

So we have seen the development of a new imperialism, and with it a return to the sorts of war and the sorts of fighting which hark back to the 1930s, as the world sank into world war. Accompanying this has gone a much more aggressive approach to war making. On 1 June 2002 George Bush delivered a speech which tore up all the rules on which international conflicts since the Second World War had been based. Addressing the graduate class at the elite West Point military academy (the US equivalent of Sandhurst), he spelt out that America had no interest in abiding by any of the previously assumed means of avoiding war. On the contrary Bush intended to hit his enemies before they could hit him:

> For much of the last century, America's defence relied on the Cold War doctrines of deterrence and containment. In some cases, these strategies still apply. But new threats also require new thinking. Deterrence – the promise of massive retaliation against nations – means nothing against shadowy terrorist networks with no nation or citizens to defend. Containment is not possible when unbalanced dictators with weapons of mass destruction can deliver those weapons on missiles or secretly provide them to terrorist allies.'
>
> We cannot defend America and our friends by hoping for the best. We cannot put our faith in the word

of tyrants, who solemnly sign non proliferation treaties, and then systematically break them. If we wait for threats to fully materialise, we will have waited too long.[1]

The speech sent a shudder through many of those who believed in negotiation rather than war. But the re-election of Bush in November 2004, alongside his immediate response to victory being the chilling claim that he had made political capital through the election campaign and now intended to spend it, caused the whole world to tremble. Here was a man who had launched two wars in his previous term, who had determined from early on to attack Iraq, who had listed Iran and North Korea in his 'axis of evil', and who had threatened among others Syria and Cuba. What was there to stop him waging war on a range of countries?

This doctrine of pre-emptive intervention served only to put the seal on a policy towards which the United States had already been moving. There were signs that the United States was increasingly impatient with the process of the United Nations during the 1990s, most notably in the decision to wage war in Kosovo in 1999 under the banner of NATO rather than the UN. The events of 11 September 2001 allowed the US government to act with impunity, and gave the doctrine the impetus that its supporters wanted. The aftermath of the attacks on New York and Washington saw most of the world's powers sign up to unconditional support for the United States in its 'war on terror'. While the initial target of this war was the Taliban regime in Afghanistan, accused of harbouring Osama bin Laden and the al Qaeda network, it rapidly became the Iraqi regime of Saddam Hussein, erstwhile friend and ally of the West but now turned into the main component of an 'axis of evil' which threatened US interests and world peace.

The blame for this change of emphasis is often placed on the 'hawks' in Washington, the right-wing neo-conservatives located at the heart of George Bush's government. While they are certainly enthusiasts for the most extreme and dangerous warmongering by the United States, and while their Project for a New American Century has played a crucial role in taking the United States down the path to war with Iraq, the ability of a small number of right-wing extremists, eccentrics and religious fundamentalists to chart government foreign policy is a symptom rather than a cause of the economic and political changes of the past two decades.

The balance sheet of Iraq demonstrates the terrible effect of the new imperialism. The country was invaded after being weakened by years of UN-imposed sanctions. The basis for the invasion as justified by the Western powers turned out to be false. There were no weapons of mass destruction in Iraq, and the basis for the war was illegal in the eyes of many, including (belatedly) the UN Secretary-General, Kofi Annan. It is now clear to most people that Bush and Blair embarked on a war to topple Saddam Hussein and to replace him with a pro-Western government in Iraq. The first bit was relatively easy: the Iraqi army controlled by a dictatorial regime was no match for the military and technological superiority of the United States backed up by the British and other powers. But the Iraqis never welcomed the foreign invaders as so many predicted: instead they began their long path to resistance almost immediately.

Their distrust of the occupiers was fuelled by hundreds of small and large incidents: the guarding of the oil ministry while museums were looted in Baghdad; the killing of demonstrators in Fallujah who were protesting at a local school being used by the US military; the frustration of having no security, no electricity and no water all too often under the occupation. Since George Bush proclaimed 'mission accomplished' on the USS

Abraham Lincoln in May 2003, the situation has deteriorated in every way. Companies, especially from the United States, like Kellogg Brown and Root and Halliburton, are making a fortune from the occupation while most Iraqis suffer. Resistance exists throughout the country; the interim government represents few apart from the occupying powers. Many are dying: over 1,000 US troops and countless Iraqis – nobody bothered to count them. But recent reports show that for every Iraqi killed by the resistance, two are killed by US forces. Civilian deaths are estimated at between 15,000 and 100,000. The onslaught on Fallujah demonstrates the barbarity of the occupation – while also failing to bring about any sort of peace.

Alongside this colonial occupation go theories which suggest that Iraqi lives are worth less than those of Americans or Europeans – witness the publicity over one Western hostage compared with the many Iraqi hostages who are ignored. Even the language is doctored: the talk is of democracy and freedom while it never explains that only US-style democracy is acceptable and only pro-US politicians are welcome in the 'international community'. 'Democracy' has become a US export as much as privatization and intellectual property – and it is rejected for the same reason. Fallujah has been destroyed, we are told, to save it for the elections. War is rarely mentioned, and resistance never – instead we are told of 'operations against insurgents'.

The occupation is bringing about exactly the situation it claims it is saving Iraqis from: growing unrest and civil war. The only solution is to pull the occupying troops out and to allow the Iraqis genuine democratic elections and the right to run their own country. The anti-war movement has campaigned on this issue since the occupation began, and support for the position has grown. It is now the official position of the British Trades Union Congress and of many major trade unions in Britain. Recent campaigns involving military families whose sons have died in Iraq have given an added urgency and poignancy to the campaign. The opposition of military families (and of serving soldiers) to the war is a new development in Britain, which has long relied on a professional army without conscription and on the loyalty engendered by such an army.

The campaign has dealt a blow to Tony Blair's war aims and has strengthened the feeling for 'troops out'. The opposition to this war by the military families is a sign of how deeply anti-war feeling has permeated British society. It could hardly be otherwise, when two million marched on 15 February 2003, when the protest against George Bush's visit to London attracted the biggest weekday demo in British history and clogged up the whole of the city, and where most people who opposed the war have not simply changed their minds.

The anti-war movement in Britain has been the most remarkable of modern times, and has now become a permanent political presence. It has provided the opposition to government policy that has been so lacking from most of our supposed elected representatives. From its inception, just after the attacks on the twin towers in New York in September 2001, the Stop the War Coalition has been marked by a diverse membership, a commitment to a core set of demands – to stop the war on terror, to oppose racism and to defend civil liberties – and an inclusive way of operating which has seen within its ranks the trade unions, peace activists, the socialist left, the Muslim community and other ethnic minorities, students, school students, pensioners and everything in between, and a high proportion of women activists, including Muslim women in hijabs.

This has produced the largest demos, but also a range of protests against the Hutton and Butler inquiries, in support of the Palestinians, against the torture of prisoners in Abu Ghraib, in defence of civil liberties and against Islamophobia. There have been thousands of public meetings, vigils, stalls and petitions putting across the anti-war message. There was mass civil disobedience on Halloween 2002 and again when war broke out in March 2003, where all round the country school students struck and demonstrated, work stopped, roads were blocked. There is a huge amount of knowledge and information among anti-war activists which has been shared and disseminated very widely. There have been debates and discussions everywhere, from union branches to mosques and churches, about the legality and propriety of the war.

All this is a sign of the determination of the anti-war movement to bring the government to account, and its refusal to move on as Tony Blair would like us to do. To those who say that we marched but didn't stop the war, it should be said that this movement is about stopping such a fundamental drive – the war on terror launched by George W Bush – that it challenges the whole basis of neo-liberal capital and is therefore a threat to its agenda. We should see Stop the War in the same mould as the US civil rights movement among blacks in the 1950s and 1960s; as the suffragette movement in Britain in the first two decades of the twentieth century, when women fought for the vote.

In that sense it is a mass movement which begins to challenge the existing politics and so takes on the colour of not just a protest movement, but one that is transformative of politics and organization, and which presents an alternative to the mainstream politics and the politicians' support for imperialist war and colonial occupation. Its story is by no means over yet, because as long as globalization breeds new and ever more deadly wars, so it will also create movements against them.

For the US military machine has an Achilles' heel in the fact that its overwhelming power breeds resistance – in Iraq and in the homelands of imperialism. Few conventional armies could take on the United States, but those fighting in Iraq, alongside the mass movements generated in the West, can create for the Americans another Vietnam, where this huge war machine loses the hearts and minds of the people of Iraq and of their own populations. Coupled with this is the mismatch between America's military power and its economic power, which is relatively less than 50 years ago. It does not have the economic muscle to provide the improvements in lives that might sweeten the pill of military intervention. Even in the United States and Britain, neo-liberalism and all it brings have always been unpopular. If the anti-capitalist movement, which is becoming more anti-imperialist, can be harnessed to the anti-war and occupation movements, there is really a force to change the world.

NOTE

1   Speech by George W Bush at West Point, 1 June 2002, published in Sifry, Micah L and Cerf, Christopher (eds) (2003) The Iraq War Reader Simon & Schuster, New York, p 269.

5 Corporate power

Olivier Hoedeman

Corporate control over the democratic process has reached unprecedented levels in all of the G8 countries, not least in the United States and Europe. As the G8 holds the key to any significant change of course in major international institutions, it is a treasured tool for big-business groupings in their efforts to preserve and consolidate the neo-liberal world order.

EUROPE DRIFTING TOWARDS US-STYLE LOBBYCRACY

Excessive levels of corporate power over US politics has been a reality for decades, including during the eight years with Clinton in the White House. The phenomena, however, has reached unprecedented dimensions since President Bush was elected in 2000. In the first four years, the Bush administration took the rewarding of corporate donors to new levels. It provided its corporate backers with extraordinary access to decision making, for instance by appointing industry lobbyists to high-level positions in US government agencies, task forces and advisory committees. Halliburton CEO Dick Cheney becoming Vice President was only the tip of the iceberg. According to a *Denver Post* article from May 2004, President Bush installed more than 100 top officials who were once corporate lobbyists or spokespeople for the very same industries they are now responsible for regulating.[1] 'The president's political appointees are making or overseeing profound changes affecting drug laws, food policies, land use, clean-air regulations and other key issues', the article concluded.

In the November 2004 elections, US business spent a record $1.2 billion in direct donations to candidates and parties. The total figure is substantially higher, as contributions to party conventions and the so-called 527 advocacy groups (such as the anti-Kerry initiative 'Swift Boat Veterans for Truth') are not included. A solid majority of the funding went to Republican Party candidates.[2] Of all industries, oil and gas corporations had the clearest party bias, and gave over 80 per cent of their donations to Republicans.[3] As the *Financial Times* pointed out in an article days after Bush's re-election and the Republicans' increased control over Congress, 'this week's election result marks the culmination of a decade-long gamble by corporate America, which has made a large bet on the Republican party'.[4] The election outcome, the *Financial Times* article predicts, 'could tilt the political landscape in favour of corporate America more dramatically than at any period in modern US history'. Indeed, the Republicans are expected to reward their corporate sponsors with a hard-line pro-business agenda. 'The Republicans are going to put their foot to the pedal', said one euphoric industry lobbyist, referring to expected policies like reinforcing corporate-controlled health care, weakening pollution standards, privatizing social security and drilling for oil in nature reserves.[5]

While the situation in the European Union has not yet reached the disastrous levels of corporate control that exist in US politics, political realities in Europe show clear signs of drifting in a similar direction. The big positive difference is the very limited role of campaign finance donations in European politics. But even without this factor, the influence of corporate lobbyists over EU policy making is significant and increasing. After decades of centralizing decision making and empowering EU institutions, EU capital Brussels has become the world's second biggest centre of lobbying (after Washington DC). Today, Brussels hosts well over 1,000 industry lobby groups, hundreds of public relations firms offering lobbying services, dozens of corporate-funded think-tanks as well as several hundred 'EU affairs' offices run by individual corporations. Of the over 15,000 professional lobbyists estimated to work in Brussels, a large majority represent large corporations, while far less than 10 per cent work for civil society groups, with far more limited financial and organizational power.

Because of the complex, often undemocratic procedures and the lack of a truly European public debate, EU decision making in Brussels generally operates in a bubble. This is bad for democracy, but provides fertile ground for corporate lobbyists and their allies in the public relations (PR) industry. In the 1990s the European Commission (with the exclusive right to propose and develop new EU legislation) was the main focus for corporate lobbyists. As the European Parliament's powers were gradually increased, this institution too has become a prime target for industry lobbyists, who have recently achieved a series of disturbing successes. Their impact is greatly increased by the uncritical attitude towards corporate lobbying that has developed in the parliament. It has for instance become routine for many MEPs to submit parliamentary amendments that were drafted by industry lobbyists. These amendments in many cases become European law. A significant number of MEPs go through the revolving door to big business after their time in the parliament. Regulations and transparency requirements on lobbying around the EU institutions are absurdly weak, far worse in fact than in the United States.[6] The new EU constitution unfortunately does little to stop these alarming trends.

Beyond concerns for democracy, the power of industry lobby groups is a serious obstacle to much-needed progress in EU social and environmental legislation. A recent example is the decision making on a new set of EU regulations for chemicals (REACH), around which EU and US industry groups have launched what is probably the biggest-ever lobby campaign in Europe. The result is a dramatically weakened REACH, full of loopholes for toxic chemicals. As a result of the shift to the right in the United States and many EU countries, industry lobby groups that for years added heavy doses of greenwash to their lobbying messages are now doing more aggressive, unapologetic anti-environmental lobbying. The European employers' federation UNICE and the European Round Table of Industrialists (ERT), for instance, have recently kicked off a new campaign to make the European Union reconsider its commitment to the Kyoto protocol for fighting climate change. PR companies eagerly help corporate clients manipulate the political process, for instance by designing fake citizens' or scientific organizations that lobby on legislation of interest to industry. One recent example is the Bromine Science Environment Forum (BSEF), a front group set up by PR giant Burson-Marsteller on behalf of a coalition of chemical companies that want to prevent a ban on the highly toxic brominated flame retardants.

The stranglehold of corporate lobby groups over the European Union's political process is boosted by the collective obsession among European politicians with becoming the world's most competitive economic bloc by 2010, the so-called Lisbon Agenda agreed in 2000. Industry groups now play the competitiveness card whichever issue they are lobbying on, and with increasing success. Moreover, following campaigning by UNICE and the ERT, EU governments have agreed to introduce so-called business impact assessments for all existing and new EU policies. The EU's Kyoto commitments for fighting climate change are first in line to be reassessed, which may further weaken efforts to combat climate change. José Manuel Barroso, who became head of a new European Commission team in November 2004, has announced that the Lisbon competitiveness goals will get absolute priority during his presidency.

THE EUROPEAN UNION'S CORPORATE-DRIVEN TRADE POLICIES

It would be wrong to interpret the growing corporate control over EU policies as simply a matter of big business lobbyists imposing their will on helpless political decision makers. In fact, EU officials often actively seek corporate guidance to shape policies. This is clearly the case with the EU's international trade policies, including its approach to negotiations in the World Trade Organization (WTO). In stark contrast to its self-proclaimed goals of 'harnessed, equitable globalization', the powerful European Commission consistently promotes the interests of EU multinational corporations.[7] Behind a veil of sustainable development rhetoric, the Commission pursues a corporate-driven, market-access agenda inimical to the interests of the world's poor and environmental sustainability. In the last ten years, inspired by the way trade negotiations are done in the United States and Japan, the European Commission has developed a deeply undemocratic addiction to alliances with big business.

During preparations for the current round of the controversial General Agreement on Trade in Services (GATS) negotiations, which started in 2000, the Commission asked the European services industry to organize itself into a lobby group comparable to the powerful US Coalition of Service Industries (USCSI). The European Services Forum (ESF) was born. Barclays Bank,

PricewaterhouseCoopers, water giant Suez and numerous other large European multinationals came together with far-reaching support from then Trade Commissioner Leon Brittan and his staff. A high-level official from the Commission's trade directorate told industry representatives, 'The European Commission is ... going to rely heavily on the European Services Forum.... We are going to rely on it just as heavily as on member state direct advice in trying to formulate our objectives.'[8]

These were not empty words. The ESF and individual services corporations played a crucial role in forming the European Union's list of demands for services liberalization presented to other WTO member states in July 2002. A leak of confidential EU documents in February 2003 revealed that the European Commission has asked no less than 72 WTO member states to open up their water sectors to international competition. This means, in effect, accelerating privatization and making it irreversible.[9]

GATS is not the only avenue by which the European Union is advancing the interests of Suez, Veolia, Thames Water and other Europe-based water corporations. The EU Water Fund, presented at the G8 summit in Evian (June 2003) is built around the flawed idea of subsidizing the expansion of private water corporations with aid money.

Another example of the privileged power arrangements that have grown between the European Commission and big business is the Transatlantic Business Dialogue (TABD), a forum for powerhouse multinationals to advise and influence transatlantic trade and regulatory policies. Since 1995, the largest EU and US-based corporations have worked closely with the Commission and the US government through the TABD to remove 'obstacles to transatlantic trade' and boost EU–US powers within the WTO. The TABD has also done its best to delay, water down, and block environmental and consumer protection legislation in Europe. Activist groups have met annual TABD conferences in Cincinnati (2000), Stockholm (2001) and Chicago (2002) with demonstrations, counter-summits, and other protests. In defence of its far-reaching support for the TABD, the European Commission cites parallel consumer, environment and labour dialogues, conveniently neglecting to mention that these never had any powers comparable to the TABD's. The Commission also fails to mention that the environment and labour dialogues ceased to exist years ago.

The European Commission has ulterior motives for its deep devotion to the TABD. The group can help merge EU–US business positions on WTO issues, resulting in a formidable joint EU–US government agenda in WTO negotiations. What other government can block such a force? The function of the TABD is therefore complementary to the G8 process, which is intended to build consensus among the world's most powerful industrialized nations. Without agreement within the G8, multilateral action of any kind is virtually impossible. If the G8 governments see eye to eye, action is virtually unstoppable. Big business is entirely aware of this reality, and uses its privileged access to exploit it to the fullest, for instance in its campaign for consolidating and deepening neo-liberal trade agreements.

THE G8: CONSOLIDATING CORPORATE POWER

The G8 include all the powerful Northern governments that dominate the WTO and intend to keep things that way. While diverging agendas often prevent consensus from emerging among the world's trade giants, G8 summits have at several key occasions in the 1980s and 1990s provided breakthroughs in stalled international trade talks.[10] These deals made among the G8 governments were effectively imposed on the rest of the

GATT/WTO member countries. The original G7 countries have since 1981 had a permanent structure in place for ensuring coordination of their trade negotiating positions, the so-called Quadrilateral Group (or Quad). Since the WTO's Seattle summit, the Quad (the European Union, the United States, Canada and Japan) have been less high-profile than before, but they continue to function on the level of trade officials.[11] Civil society groups around the world reject these undemocratic and exclusive forums for pre-cooking WTO outcomes. For big business, which de facto controls trade policy making in all the G8 capitals, the G8 and the Quad are of course ideal arrangements.

In addition to controlling national government and EU trade policies, big business also has direct, privileged access to the G8 summits. The Paris-based International Chamber of Commerce (ICC), as the *Global Accountability Report* points out:

> has unparalleled access to G7 summits. Every year, the host government of the G7 summit confers with the ICC presidency on the eve of the event. This consultation has proved to be a highly effective means of channelling business recommendations to the summit leaders.[12]

The ICC, founded in 1919, is the single largest and most influential international corporate lobby group. This self-proclaimed 'world business organization' has thousands of member companies in over 130 countries.[13] It is dominated by the world's most powerful transnational corporations, including Dupont, Vivendi Universal, Unilever, Volvo and Nestlé. The political clout of its members has secured it unparalleled access not only to the G8, but also to other key economic and political institutions in the global economy, including the WTO and the United Nations.[14]

The ICC's top priority is to consolidate, expand and deepen neo-liberal trade rules, particularly the WTO system which it helped design. It is therefore no surprise that it used the occasion of the last G8 summit (Sea Island, Georgia, USA, June 2004) to push for speeding up WTO talks, as well as calling for the launch of controversial investment negotiations.[15] On 10 May 2004, an ICC delegation delivered a statement to George W Bush, who was to host the G8 Summit at Sea Island. 'We call upon the G8 heads to renew their pledge to take the lead in bringing the WTO round to a successful and early conclusion, and to commit themselves personally to that goal', the statement said.[16]

The ICC frequently uses its recommendations to the G8 to launch attacks on the global justice movement and its demands for progressive regulation of transnational corporations and global markets. Before the 2001 G8 summit in Genoa, for instance, the ICC insisted that 'governments should reject demands by publicly unaccountable and frequently unrepresentative external groups that seek to impose codes of conduct on multinationals'.[17] The ICC delegation that met with French President Jacques Chirac of France in advance of the G8 meeting in Evian (June 2003) called the G8 to 'uphold the voluntary nature of corporate responsibility initiatives'.[18] This demand was part of the ICC's counter-campaign, aiming to kill off the proposed United Nations Norms on Business and Human Rights, with self-proclaimed corporate social responsibility (CSR) champion Shell in a leading role.

The Norms aim to make the human rights obligations of transnational corporations explicit, and suggest further steps towards corporate accountability. The ICC's efforts to sideline the Norms were led by Robin Aram, Shell's Vice-President of External Relations and Policy Development and head of the ICC's Commission on 'Business in Society'. Shell wants free hands to decide its choices on how to weigh 'people, planet and profits', to the extent that it takes the lead in campaigning against the Norms, in alliance with the most reactionary parts of international business. As a result of the corporate offensive, governments attending the annual meeting of the UN Commission on Human Rights (Geneva, March 2004) did not endorse the Norms. The US government especially was instrumental in sending the Norms back to the UN Sub-Commission for the Protection and Promotion of Human Rights, causing delay and uncertainty about the future of the initiative.

CHALLENGING THE G8

On the one hand the effectiveness of the G8 as a tool for advancing corporate agendas should not be overestimated: diverging positions among the world's most powerful governments often result in summit conclusions that contain little real meaning behind the diplomatic wording. At the same time, at key occasions deals made between the G8 countries have had far-reaching impacts, for instance in pushing through corporate-biased trade deals. And importantly, while it is hardly a world government, very little happens in international institutions without the previous consent of the G8. For the much-needed shift towards an international agenda that prioritizes global economic justice and environmental sustainability, the corporate-controlled G8 is a major obstacle. This is why the struggle against the G8 (its policies and its illegitimacy as a global power broker) is so essential for the global justice movement.

NOTES

1   'When advocates become regulators', *Denver Post*, 23 May 2004. The article contains detailed profiles of former industry lobbyists who are now

helping US government agencies shape regulatory and other policies for the industries that once employed them.

2   See '2004 election overview: business-labor-ideology split in PAC & individual donations to candidates and parties',
    <http://www.opensecrets.org/overview/blio.asp?cycle=2004>.

3   '2004 election overview: top industries',
    <http://www.opensecrets.org/overview/industries.asp?cycle=2004>.

4   'Foot to the pedal: US business expects a clear run from a second Bush term', *Financial Times*, 5 November 2004.

5   Ibid.

6   The register of lobbyists with a full-time access pass to the European Parliament only lists name and organization, not who these people (many of them professional lobby consultants) are lobbying for, on what issue and how much money is involved. In the United States, at least, the 1996 Lobbying Disclosure Act obliges lobbyists to register when they start lobbying on a new issue, to report who their clients are and what budget they have for lobbying on the issue. Also, all lobby groups have to submit a report twice per year, describing this type of information. Clearly the Lobbying Disclosure Act has failed to prevent further increase of industry control over decision making, but this is mainly a result of weak implementation as well as the power that big business continues to exercise through campaign finance. In Europe, this kind of regulation seems a necessary first step to roll back excessive corporate lobbying influence. It will allow parliamentarians to better know who they are being lobbied by, enable media to increase their scrutiny of corporate lobbying campaigns, and also provide civil society with a potent tool for counter-campaigning.

7   In WTO negotiations, the European Union is represented by the European Commission, and in particular DG Trade.

8   Madelin, Robert (1999) 'Preparing for GATS 2000: the European Commission approach', speech at the conference How to Open Services Markets Worldwide, London, 21 September.

9   The Commission drew up its liberalization wish-list concerning water delivery in close consultation with Veolia (Vivendi), Suez, RWE (Thames Water), and other giant private water corporations.

10 For instance the G8 summits in Tokyo (1986), Houston (1990) and Tokyo (1993). See Ullrich, Heidi (2004) 'Effective or defective? The G8 and multilateral trade negotiations', London School of Economics and Political Science, March. The paper provides an interesting overview,

but entirely lacks criticism of neo-liberal trade policies as well as of the role of the G8.

11 Since 1999 there has been no trade ministers summit of the Quad countries, but trade officials continue to meet frequently to fine-tune their cooperation. See Ullrich (2004) (note 10).

12 One World Trust (2003) *Power Without Accountability: The Global Accountability Report 2003*, One World Trust, London.

13 See <www.iccwbo.org>.

14 The ICC is a prominent partner in Kofi Annan's Global Compact between the United Nations and transnational corporations, launched in January 2000. The total absence of monitoring and enforcement mechanisms makes the Compact an ideal 'greenwash' instrument. The partnership with the United Nations should be taken in context with the group's long and ongoing history of vigorously lobbying to weaken international environmental treaties, including the Kyoto protocol to curb climate change, the Convention on Biodiversity and the Basel Convention against trade in toxic waste.

15 'Top western firms urge relaunch of stalled trade liberalisation talks', Agence France Presse, 15 May 2004.

16 'Business groups unite in pressing G8 to boost Doha trade round', <http://www.iccwbo.org/home/news_archives/2003/stories/brt.asp>.

17 'G8 must cooperate more closely to improve financial stability', <http://www.iccwbo.org/home/news_archives/2001/stability.asp>.

18 'Business calls on the G8 leaders to set aside disagreements over Iraq and work together', <http://www.iccwbo.org/home/news_archives/2003/stories/g8.asp>.

6 The Gang of 8:
the good governance roadshow

Emma Miller

INTRODUCTION

The G8 is coming to Scotland in 2005. Top billing in the G8 roadshow goes to Africa, which has been identified as a critical case. The G8's prescription for the African continent incorporates good governance, installing democracy and development. This may sound like good medicine, but there is reason to believe that the G8 consists of quacks. This is worrying because the wrong diagnosis will make Africa's condition worse.

The G8 focus on the activities of African leaders deflects attention from the global economy, the key cause of poverty and conflict in the continent. The potential for positive input is immense, as the global economy is controlled by the G8. However, far from promoting democracy and good governance in Africa, the G8's free market reforms impede good governance, promote corruption and weaken democracy.

This chapter considers the real role of the G8 in relation to Africa. To get the measure of the Gang of 8, we should first examine their credentials. This necessitates consideration of their domestic governance records, particularly promoting democracy, respecting human rights and observing international law. The lesser-known G8 leaders are included here as they all play a part. What emerges is a gang with an impressive criminal profile including corruption, illegal war and crimes against humanity. If we consider the evidence that they are not just quacks, but crooks to boot, their ability to prescribe for Africa is seriously called into question.

G8 CRIMES

Three key themes will be covered in considering G8 crimes: illegal war, human rights abuses and corruption. First, we should consider the character of the top dog, George W Bush. Bush was already known to be an enthusiastic executioner when he seized the presidency of the United States in 2000 – having signed more death warrants (113) than any other elected official alive today in the United States. Now bolstered by his heavyweight homeboys when in the States – the Neocons – Bush has a strong hold over the Gang of 8. While some gang members have questioned his more murderous actions, most of them continue to fall over each other to curry favour with the boss. Bush's homeboys are seriously to the right of just about anyone you can think of – and are capable of anything in their pursuit of US interests. And yet the crusade for oil and profits is sold as promoting democracy. This brings us to the first theme.

Illegal war

Bush is primarily responsible for the illegal war in Iraq, which by November 2004 had resulted in the deaths of over 100,000 Iraqi civilians. Bush told his people that the war was necessary to protect them from terrorism, following attacks on New York's twin towers on 11 September 2001, even though Iraq's Saddam Hussein had no connection with the attacks. While most G8 leaders recognized that the war was globally unpopular, and initially tried to maintain some distance, Tony Blair threw caution to the wind and provided the fig-leaf for the Iraq war. Blair lied to his people because the boss wanted back-up. The future does not look entirely rosy for Blair as a result. The Athens Bar Association in 2003 declared that it would file a suit against Britain at the International Criminal Court (ICC). And in 2004 it was announced that Welsh nationalist MP Adam Price would initiate an attempt to impeach Blair for 'causing injury to the state', 'breaching his constitutional duties' and 'lying' to Parliament on Iraq. Other G8 leaders provided support for the war, most notably Berlusconi, but also Martin, Koizumi and Putin.

Human rights abuses

Human rights appear from time to time on the G8 bandwagon. Previously, in Okinawa in July 2000, the Miyazaki Initiative on Conflict Prevention was adopted by G8 foreign ministers. This stated that 'efforts to prevent conflict must be based upon observance of international law, including the UN charter, democracy, respect for human rights, the rule of law, good governance, sustainable development and other fundamental values, which constitute the foundation of international peace and security'.[1] The G8 tune has changed both domestically and internationally. Since 2001, some G8 members have used the anti-terror campaign to curb civil liberties and tighten punitive policies against asylum seekers. The United States and the United Kingdom have introduced measures permitting prolonged arbitrary detention without adequate judicial review of foreigners suspected of terrorist activity. Further, Amnesty

International has argued that Washington's 'war mentality' has led it down a slippery slope toward disregard for the rule of law, resulting in torture in Iraq and alleged abuse in Afghanistan and at Guantanamo Bay.[2]

Putin has endeared himself to the boss by reclassifying Russia's conflict with the separatist republic of Chechnya as part of the war on terror. Bush has since accorded Putin status as 'a stalwart in the fight against terror'.[3] In fact, Russia's appalling human rights record in the breakaway republic and the short-sightedness of the military solution envisioned by Putin are disastrous. Meanwhile other G8 leaders rationalize such human rights abuses in the name of fighting terrorism. In the days following 9/11, German Chancellor Schroeder and Italian Prime Minister Berlusconi called for a 'reassessment' of Russia's abusive actions in Chechnya.[4]

Corruption

The G8 leaders have got a lot of work to do on their own turf before tackling corruption in Africa. Whether you define corruption as putting the interests of corporations before those of your people, or as having a hand in the till (or both), the G8 has plenty of experience. All eight leaders have established neo-liberal credentials. In Germany the shift came in 1998 with the election of Schroeder. The new leader quickly set about dismantling the German model of 'Rhineland capitalism' which had placed more emphasis on the social-welfare state than some G8 partners. Using the model of Britain's New Labour, Schroeder proceeded with big tax cuts for business and 'Agenda 2010' – a programme attacking the welfare state.[5] While the reforms have been welcomed by the international financial institutions and foreign investors, they will force many Germans below the poverty line.[6]

[93]

Two G8 leaders are sheltering behind their presidential positions to avoid trials for corruption. Berlusconi, the richest man in Italy, has faced numerous charges of corruption. He drove a law through parliament in June 2003, giving himself and four other top officials immunity from prosecution while in office. This halted his corruption trial in Milan, where he stood accused of bribing judges. Prosecutors at the aborted trial denounced the law as 'unconstitutional'. Chirac was accused of corruption during his time as Mayor of Paris and as president of the Gaullist RPR Party. Judges were recently thwarted in pursuing corruption charges by Chirac's claim to presidential immunity, causing one of them to resign in disgust.

So we see that all eight gang members are engaged in promoting their own interests and those of corporations before their own people. Yet their crimes include examples of the very subjects on which they presume to preach to African leaders. Further, their slavish devotion to corporations is evident in their actions on Africa.

G8'S ACTION FOR AFRICA

It has been our experience that reliable institutions and governance are a precondition for long-term or large-scale private investment.

(G8 Africa Action Plan)[7]

This section concerns the G8's 2002 *Africa Action Plan*. Central to the plan is the concept of good governance. We already know there is considerable irony in the G8's presumption to preach on this topic, given their own records of governance. Among the other prescriptions for Africa are democracy and development. However, the statement above touches on key contradictions in associated policy. The G8 view of 'democracy' is increasingly associated with African leaders' willingness to promote the neo-liberal agenda, and the related assumption is that neo-liberalism will in turn promote development, despite overwhelming evidence to the contrary.

The G8's public pronouncements present the African continent as a heavy burden – as a 'scar on the conscience' as Blair would have it. However, the baseline priority in setting policy on Africa is the commercial interests of the rich countries, and this involves placing and keeping in power leaders keen to cooperate with that agenda. The conflict between the promotion of corporate interests and the goal of development is a key theme here, with brief examples of how this relates to agriculture, arms and health. The contradiction between the professed aims and actions of the G8 will be revisited in the concluding section, which considers African priorities. First, we can consider examples of the corporate priorities of the G8 in Africa.

Paul Martin became leader of Canada relatively recently (in 2004) compared with the other G8 leaders. He soon made his allegiance to neo-liberalism clear in defining Canada's place in the world: 'More than ever, our prosperity and security – the quality of life in our communities and the strength of our families – depends on our ability to access markets, to compete with determination and resourcefulness.'[8] Similarly, Schroeder's priorities were revealed in his first official tour of Africa in January 2004, by a delegation including business leaders such as the CEOs of Deutsche Telekom, Commerzbank, DaimlerChrysler, Lufthansa and others focused on Africa's profit potential.

The commercial interest in Africa is intense. Blair and Berlusconi, for example, emphasize 'fostering Africa's inclusion into the global economy'. While they view aid as an 'essential tool' in development, the emphasis is on private investment and the Economic Partnership Agreements planned for 2007: 'The

EPAs ... would liberalise trade between Europe and Africa, foster Africa's regional integration and create wider African markets which would be far more attractive to foreign investments and enable greater exploitation of domestic resources.'[9]

While the G8 emphasize investment as a development tool for Africa, it is the populations of African countries who pay the price when their leaders concentrate on investors. South African research company BusinessMap ranks countries according to the 'risk factors' scrutinized by potential investors: extent of privatization, labour and infrastructure costs, political stability and transaction costs.[10] The development and promotion of corporate interests take precedence over development of decent life conditions for African people: 'To attract investors, countries compete to lower costs. That can mean offering cheap labour, weak environmental laws, lax health and safety standards or reduced social services. The lower your standards, the higher the investment.'[11]

Additionally, individual G8 leaders can demand favours for investment support. In 2004 Koizumi urged the heads of African states to devise 'sound industrial policies' to attract investment from Asia. The additional, not particularly democratic, string attached was that Japan expected African nations to back Tokyo's bid for a permanent seat on the UN Security Council.[12]

Among the development areas identified in the Africa Action Plan are agriculture and health. Agriculture is highlighted as central to the 'quality of life of most Africans', and on health, there is recognition that malaria, tuberculosis and AIDS 'remain as obstacles to Africa's development.'[13] However, the commitment of the G8 to their own commercial interests repeatedly undermines the developmental goals set out in the Action Plan. The undemocratic control of the G8 boss is also evident here. Despite constantly pressuring African states to practise free trade, the Bush administration refuses to stop subsidizing exports to the continent. Similarly, the EU has subsidized domestic over-production for decades, dumping the excesses on Africa, undermining production there. At the G8 summit in Evian in 2003, Blair scuppered proposals from Chirac that both the European Union and the United States should stop subsidizing exports of food to Africa. Blair (again) chose instead to do Bush's bidding.[14]

Although he has professed commitment to addressing the HIV/AIDS pandemic in Africa, Bush undermines access to affordable medicines by working to impose enhanced patent protections, for the benefit of the big pharmaceutical companies. In Evian in 2003, NGOs charged that, in order to mend relations with Bush after their rift over Iraq, Chirac sacrificed the health of AIDS victims. The NGO Health Gap said that the plan on health was weakened after interventions by the United States – to water down references to increasing access to essential medicines and the financing of the Global Fund against AIDS, malaria and tuberculosis.[15]

> Time and again, progress in Africa has been undermined or destroyed by conflict and insecurity.... Economic development has been deeply undermined as scarce resources needed to fight poverty have too often been wasted in deadly and costly armed conflicts. We are determined to make conflict prevention and resolution a top priority.[16]

The arms race during the Cold War in the 1970s and 1980s, involving the poorest regions, is arguably the foundation for their poverty today.[17] Arms purchases often diverted budgets for development. Good governance has not been a consideration for Western arms vendors. G8 governments have armed some of the world's worst abusers of human rights. Even now, despite being locked into the poverty trap of debt, the poorest nations are still regarded as profitable arms customers. At least two-thirds of all global arms transfers between 1997 and 2001 came from five members of the G8: the United States, Russia, France, the United Kingdom and Germany. These countries, as well as the other members of the G8 – Italy and Canada – all have varying laws requiring that military exports be licensed. Japan officially prohibits military exports. Yet in each case, these controls have been ineffective, or bypassed.[18]

CONCLUSION

The G8 consists of eight leaders whose records both domestically and internationally are fatally flawed, and fundamentally damaging to the world. They continue to profess commitment to 'promoting good governance', 'democracy' and 'development' in Africa. However a brief glance at their records demonstrates how unqualified they are to preach these messages. While some prominent African leaders have bought into their neo-liberal mindset, they are not representative of the continent's people.

Three African leaders – Mbeki of South Africa, Bouteflika of Algeria and Obasanjo of Nigeria – came up with the 'New Partnership for Africa's Development' (NEPAD) in 2002. Though promoted as an African initiative, it is telling that it was consecrated at the Kananaskis G8 summit that year. Although NEPAD's architects emphasized the role of African civil society in the plan, there has been little evidence of this.[19] Prominent Soweto community activist Trevor Ngwane argues that social justice activists across Africa see NEPAD as a legitimacy-booster – 'for Mbeki who is failing at home on many fronts, and for the G8 leaders, whose disastrous international economic policies require a front-man from the global South'.[20]

The G8 released their *Africa Action Plan* – as a response to NEPAD – in 2002, with the promise of US$6 billion to support it. A year later, after the G8 summit in Evian, representatives of six of the largest African NGOs and national networks issued a statement on G8 delivery: 'The outcome of the 2003 G8 Summit has been stunning on its failure to make progress on the debt, health, trade and agriculture issues.'[21] The G8 Summit closed with offers of assistance in the range of less than 1 per cent of what was spent on the war in Iraq.

The most recent Blair spin initiative is the Commission for Africa, announced in early 2004, bringing together 17 international and African players, including Bob Geldof, who has described Bush as 'the champion of the poor'.[22] When the second meeting of the commission took place in October 2004, several of the African leaders who might have been expected to attend were missing, choosing to be in Senegal for a meeting of African intellectuals. Meanwhile the commission was given a mere seven months to report, left in the hands of civil servants – mostly drafted in with little knowledge about the continent.[23]

The G8 argue that critics of their PR initiatives on Africa are cynical whingers who fail to produce alternatives. That is false. The basic policy shifts required to give Africa a break are not rocket science and are achievable. They can be distilled from the priorities of the African NGOs mentioned above, as well as Western NGOs like the World Development Movement,[24] and include the following; cancel the debts, make trade fair, tax financial speculation, cut arms supplies, stop promoting privatization, regulate multinationals, increase aid to 0.7 per cent of GDP, enable African countries to promote food sovereignty, and cut greenhouse gas emissions which are causing climate chaos. These measures would do more to prevent terrorism than any amount of repressive legislation and warmongering, the current responses favoured by the G8.

They should get on with it.

NOTES

1   Human Rights Watch (2002) Human Rights in Security and Development:Recommendations for the G8 Summit, June 2002, including the G8's Action Plan for Africa, 5 June
    <http://www.hrw.org/backgrounder/g8/g8mem0605.htm>.

2   Amnesty International (2004) 'USA: Pattern of brutality and cruelty – war crimes at Abu Ghraib', press release, 5 July
    <http://news.amnesty.org/index/ENGAMR510772004>.

3   Starobin, P (2003) 'Chechnya: Putin's peace plan seems doomed to backfire', Business Week online, 21 July,
    <http://zdnet.businessweek.com/magazine/content/03_29/b3842070_mz015.htm>.

4   Human Rights Watch (2002) (see note 1).

5   Wahl, P (2003) 'The end of Rhineland capitalism: Germany at the crossroads', Red Pepper, 29 December,
    <http://www.redpepper.org.uk/Jan2004/x-Jan2004-Wahl.html>.

6   Connolly, K (2004) 'Berlin hits back as anti-reform protests spread east', Daily Telegraph, 10 August,
    <http://www.portal.telegraph.co.uk/news/main.jhtml?xml=/news/2004/08/10/wgerm10.xml&sSheet=/news/2004/08/10/ixworld.html>.

7   G8 (2002) Africa Action Plan
    <http://www.state.gov/e/eb/rls/othr/11515.htm>.

8   Martin, P (2004) 'Prime Minister's reply to the speech from the throne', Office of the Prime Minister, Government of Canada, 5 January,
    <http://pm.gc.ca/eng/sft-ddt.asp?id=2>.

9   UK–Italy summit, London, 13 July 2004, Government of Italy,
    <http://www.governo.it/GovernoInforma/Dossier/vertice_italo_britannico_2004/REV%203-0907041(comunicato).pdf>.

10 BBC online (2002) 'Investors wary of southern Africa', BBC Online, 4 February, <http://news.bbc.co.uk/1/hi/business/1800625.stm>.

11 New Internationalist (2004) 'Race to the bottom', New Internationalist no 374, December.

12 Karasaki, T (2004) 'Koizumi calls on African leaders to draw investment', Asahi, 2 November,
    < http://www.asahi.com/english/politics/TKY200411020111.html>.

13 G8 (2002) (see note 7).

14 Monbiot, G (2003) 'Blair trashes Africa', Guardian, 3 June
    <http://www.monbiot.com/archives/2003/06/03/blair-trashes-africa>.

15 Fabricius, P (2003) 'Chirac places Bush ahead of Africa', The Star,
    <http://www.thestar.co.za/
    index.php?fSectionId=132&fArticleId=163372>.

16 G8 (2002) (see note 7).

17 Burrows, Gideon (2003) The No-Nonsense Guide to the International Arms Trade, New Internationalist, Oxford; G8 (2002) (see note 7).

18 Amnesty International (2003) 'A catalogue of failures: G8 countries arm human rights violators', press release, 19 May,
    <http://web.amnesty.org/library/index/engior300032003>.

19 Human Rights Watch, 2002 (see note 1).

20 Ngwane, T (2002) 'A new partnership for Africa's development or just more Washington-friendly economics?' WDM in Action, Summer.

21 African NGOs (2003) Joint statement from African NGOs and trade unions as the G8 summit comes to an end in Evian, 3 June, World Development Movement
    <http://www.wdm.org.uk/campaign/evianafricanngo.htm>.

22 Monbiot, G (2004) 'Exploitation on tap', Guardian online, 19 October,
    <http://www.guardian.co.uk/southafrica/story/
    0,13262,1330423,00.html>.

23 Dowden, R (2004) 'Can the Tony and Bob Show really do any good for Africa?' Independent online, 5 October,
    <http://news.independent.co.uk/world/africa/story.jsp?story=568923>.

24 WDM (2004) 'Blair's Africa commission is 'unnecessary diversion from real action for Africa', press release, 29 April,
    <http://www.wdm.org.uk/presrel/current/africacommission.htm>.

Section Two
Issues

7 Climate change[1]

George Monbiot

In common with all those generations that have contemplated catastrophe, we appear to be incapable of understanding what confronts us: the threat of climate change.

Three wholly unexpected sets of findings now suggest that the problem could be much graver than anyone had imagined. Work by the Nobel laureate Paul Crutzen suggests that the screening effect produced by particles of soot and smoke in the atmosphere is stronger than climatologists thought: one variety of manmade filth, in other words, has been protecting us from the effects of another.[2] As ancient smokestacks are closed down or replaced with cleaner technology, climate change, paradoxically, will intensify.

At the same time, rising levels of carbon dioxide appear to be breaking down the world's peat bogs. Research by Chris Freeman at the University of Bangor shows that the gas stimulates bacteria which dissolve the peat.[3] Peat bogs are more or less solid carbon. When they go into solution the carbon turns into carbon dioxide, which in turn dissolves more peat. The bogs of Europe, Siberia and North America, the *New Scientist* reports, contain the equivalent of 70 years of global industrial carbon emissions.[4]

Worse still are the possible effects of changes in cloud cover. Until recently climatologists assumed that, because higher temperatures would raise the rate of evaporation, more clouds would form. By blocking some of the heat from the sun they would reduce the rate of global warming. But now it seems that higher temperatures may instead burn off the clouds. Research by Bruce Wielicki of NASA suggests that some parts of the tropics are already less cloudy than they were in the 1980s.[5]

The result of all this is that the maximum temperature rise proposed by the Intergovernmental Panel on Climate Change in 2001 may be a grave underestimate.[6] Rather than a possible 5.8 degrees of warming this century, we could be looking at a maximum of 10 or 12.[7] Goodbye, kind world.

Like every impending disaster this one has generated a voluble industry of denial. Few people are now foolish enough to claim that man-made climate change isn't happening at all, but the few are still granted plenty of scope to make idiots of themselves in public.

The *Mail on Sunday* and its Nobel laureate-in-waiting, Peter Hitchens informed his readers in 2001 that 'the greenhouse effect probably doesn't exist'. 'There is as yet no evidence for it.'[8] Perhaps Mr Hitchens would care to explain why our climate differs from that of the moon. That some of the heat from the sun is trapped in the earth's atmosphere by gases (the greenhouse effect) has been established since the mid-nineteenth century. But, like most of these nincompoops, Hitchens claims to be defending science from its opponents. 'The only reason these facts are so little-known', he tells us, is (apart from the reason that he has just made them up), 'that a self-righteous love of "the environment" has now replaced religion as the new orthodoxy.'[9]

Hitchens, in turn, is an Einstein beside that famous climate scientist, Melanie Phillips. Writing in the *Daily Mail* in January 2004, she dismissed the entire canon of climatology as 'a global fraud' perpetrated by the 'leftwing, anti-American, anti-West ideology which goes hand in hand with anti-globalisation and the belief that everything done by the industrialised world is wicked.'[10] This belief must be shared by the Pentagon, whose report pictures climate change as the foremost threat to global security.[11] In an earlier article, she claimed that 'most independent climate specialists, far from supporting [global warming], are deeply sceptical.'[12] She managed to name only one, however, and he receives his funding from the fossil fuel industry.[13] Having blasted the world's climatologists for 'scientific illiteracy', she then trumpeted her own. The latest report by the Intergovernmental Panel on Climate Change (which collates the findings of climatologists) is, she complained, 'studded with weasel words' such as 'very likely' and 'best estimate'.[14] These weasel words are, of course, what make it a scientific report, rather than a column by Melanie Phillips.

But these two dolts are rather less dangerous than the BBC, and its insistence on 'balancing' its coverage of climate change. It appears to be incapable of running an item on the subject without inviting a sceptic to comment on it. Usually this is either someone from a corporate-funded think-tank (who is, of course, never introduced as such) or the professional anti-environmentalist Philip Stott. Professor Stott is a retired biogeographer. Like almost all the prominent sceptics he has never published a peer-reviewed paper on climate change. But he has made himself available to dismiss climatologists' peer-reviewed work as the 'lies' of eco-fundamentalists.[15] This wouldn't be so objectionable if the BBC made it clear that these people are not climatologists, and the overwhelming majority of qualified scientific opinion is against them. Instead, it leaves us with the impression that professional opinion is split down the middle.

Now these twits have been joined by the former environmentalist David Bellamy. Writing in the British tabloid the *Daily Mail,* Bellamy asserted that 'the link between the burning of fossil fuels and global warming is a myth.'[16] Like almost all the climate change deniers, he based his claim on a petition produced in 1998 by the Oregon Institute of Science and Medicine and 'signed by over 18,000 scientists'. Had Bellamy studied the signatories, he would have discovered that the 'scientists' include Ginger Spice and the cast of MASH.[17] The Oregon Institute is run by a fundamentalist Christian called Arthur Robinson. Its petition was attached to what purported to be a scientific paper, printed in the font and format of the Proceedings of the National Academy of Sciences. In fact, the paper had not been peer reviewed or published in any scientific journal.[18] Anyone could sign the petition, and anyone did: only a handful of the signatories are experts in climatology,[19] and quite a few of them appear to have believed that they were signing a genuine paper.[20] And yet, six years later, this petition is still being wheeled out to suggest that climatologists say global warming isn't happening.

But most of those who urge inaction have given up denying the science, and now seek instead to suggest that climate change is taking place, but it's no big deal. Their champion is the Danish statistician Bjorn Lomborg. Writing in the British broadsheet *The Times* in May 2004, Lomborg claimed to have calculated that global warming will cause US$5 trillion of damage, and would cost US$4 trillion to ameliorate.[21] The money, he insisted, would be better spent elsewhere.

The idea that we can attach a single meaningful figure to the costs incurred by global warming is laughable. Climate change is a non-linear process, whose likely impacts cannot be totted up like the expenses for a works outing to the seaside. Even those outcomes we can predict are impossible to cost. We now know, for example, that the Himalayan glaciers which feed the Ganges, the Bramaputra, the Mekong, the Yangtze and the other great Asian rivers are likely to disappear within 40 years.[22] If these rivers dry up during the irrigation season, then the rice production which currently feeds over one third of humanity collapses, and the world goes into net food deficit. If Lomborg believes he can put a price on that, he has plainly spent too much of his life with his calculator and not enough with human beings.

What makes all this so dangerous is that it plays into the hands of the corporate lobbyists. A leaked memo written by Frank Luntz, the US Republican and corporate strategist, warned his party that:

> The environment is probably the single issue on which Republicans in general – and President Bush in particular – are most vulnerable.... Should the public come to believe that the scientific issues are settled, their views about global warming will change accordingly. Therefore, you need to continue to make the lack of scientific certainty a primary issue in the debate.[23]

At the 2005 G8 summit, Tony Blair has promised to make climate change one of the key issues. As it approaches, we can expect more and more mud to be flung at climatologists and the environmentalists who promote their findings. Blair himself will be torn between his need to be seen to keep his promises and his need to keep appeasing George Bush. The fossil fuel lobby, with the help of a pliant media, will do all it can to ensure that he doesn't jeopardize the special relationship, by making an issue out of the minor inconvenience of the death of the planet.

NOTES

1   Adapted from columns originally published in the *Guardian* 27 April and 10 August 2004.
2   *New Scientist* (2003) 'Heat will soar as haze fades', 178:2398, 7 June.

3   Pearce, Fred (2004) 'Peat bogs harbour carbon time bomb', *New Scientist*, 183:2455, 10 July.

4   Ibid.

5   Pearce, Fred (2004) 'Harbingers of doom?' *New Scientist*, 183:2457, 24 July.

6   Intergovernmental Panel on Climate Change (2001) *Climate Change 2001: Synthesis report, summary for policymakers*, IPCC, Geneva.

7   Fred Pearce, as note 5.

8   Hitchens, Peter (2001) 'Global warming? It's hot air and hypocrisy', *Mail on Sunday*, 29 July

9   Ibid.

10   Phillips, Melanie (2004) 'Global warming or global fraud?' *Daily Mail*, 12 January.

11   Townsend, Mark and Harris, Paul (2004) 'Now the Pentagon tells Bush: climate change will destroy us', *Observer*, 22 February

12   Phillips, Melanie (2004) 'The myth of global warming endangers the planet', *Sunday Times*, 15 April.

13   This is Professor Richard Lindzen.

14   Melanie Phillips, as note 12.

15   See for example Kirby, Alex (2002) 'Sceptics denounce climate science "lie"', BBC News Online, 25th February, <http://news.bbc.co.uk/1/hi/sci/tech/1833902.stm>.

16   Bellamy, David (2004) 'Global warming? What a load of poppycock!' *Daily Mail*, 9 July.

17   PR Watch, viewed 6 August 2004, Oregon Institute of Science and Medicine, <http://www.prwatch.org/improp/oism.html>.

18   Stevens, William K (1998) 'Science academy disputes attack on global warming', *New York Times*, 22 April.

19   Ibid.

20   Musser, George (2001) 'Climate of uncertainty: the unknowns in global warming research don't have to be showstoppers', *Scientific American*, October.

21   Lomborg, Bjorn (2004) 'Time for the climate doomsters to face reality', *The Times*, 11 May.

22   See for example *New Scientist* (2004) 'Glacier meltdown', 182:2446, 8 May; Kulkarni, Anil V, Rathore, B P and Alex, Suja (2004) 'Monitoring of glacial mass balance in the Baspa basin using accumulation area ratio method', *Current Science*, 86:1, 10 January.

23 Luntz, Frank (2002) 'The environment: a cleaner, safer, healthier America'. The leaked memo can be downloaded from the bottom of this page: <http://www.ewg.org/briefings/luntzmemo/>.

8 Trade

Susan George

If there's one thing the G8 leadership agrees on, it's the virtues of free trade. Trade has iconic status. Free trade commandments are right up there with the ones Moses received on Mount Sinai; not to be questioned by decent, right-thinking people. The first thing to understand about the free trade debate is that, as far as the G8 and other neo-liberals are concerned, there isn't one. Debate is not called for in matters of canonical doctrine and religious belief.

If we in the alter-globalization movement hope to challenge free trade dogma, we must not only confront this rigid mindset but also jog the exceedingly short historical memories of today's fiercest free trade advocates. All the G8 countries, without exception, built their present economic strength behind high tariff walls, overt protectionism and government intervention, policies now roundly condemned by those same countries that practised them most enthusiastically in order to reach their present opulent status. These countries hope to keep trade rules attuned to their advantage because the stakes are high. International trade now represents over nine trillion dollars a year (US\$9,100,000,000,000 to be precise).

Throughout the nineteenth and during much of the twentieth century, the United States, Britain and other European countries protected their infant industries from competition using tariff barriers routinely exceeding 50, even 100 per cent. Like its Western counterparts, Japan still uses tariffs plus an elaborate mix of disguised protectionist measures to make sure rival producers will be kept at bay. Later still, South Korea and the other Asian tigers erected barriers and targeted government spending towards the industrial sectors they chose to favour. None of that neo-liberal, throw-open-your-borders, the-market-knows-best nonsense for any of the rich countries, thank you.

The rules governing the World Trade Organization (WTO) ensure that the strategies consistently used by these winners are placed off-limits for the countries that have not yet arrived. They are told to seek their 'comparative' (or 'natural') advantage; to produce whatever they are most suited to producing, then to exchange these goods with other nations for what they cannot produce as efficiently at home. This eminently rational trade theory undoubtedly worked when David Ricardo first proposed it at the dawn of the nineteenth century: his classic example was England, which should produce woollen cloth because its natural advantage was based on lots of grass, sheep and weaving mills. It should exchange the said cloth with Portugal, naturally endowed with sunlight and good vine-nurturing soils, for port wine.

Two hundred years on – as many free trade enthusiasts appear not to have noticed – the world is not quite the place it was in Ricardo's day. Transport, communications and financial costs are far lower; technology has spread, many countries can and do produce exactly the same sorts of goods. Their comparative advantage frequently lies only in the domain of cheap, docile labour and dirty, wasteful production methods. Countries that do not allow trade unions, repress their labour force most efficiently and maintain the lowest environmental standards can sell more cheaply on world markets, true, but there is nothing 'natural' about such an advantage.

According to the theory, comparative advantage should favour producers of raw materials, particularly of tropical products, in much the way grape growing was a natural advantage in Portugal. Unfortunately, whereas nineteenth-century Portugal was able to make wine from its grapes, trade rules today work systematically to prevent commodity producers from processing their own raw materials. The G8 countries, all great advocates of free trade, erect barriers against processed goods in order to maintain control over the more lucrative 'value-added' activities, like turning cocoa beans into chocolate. India, for example, processes only 1 per cent of the food it grows, whereas the United States processes 70 per cent of its home-grown food. Rich-country tariffs on fully processed foods are at least twice as high as those applied to imported foodstuffs that have undergone little or no processing.

Rich, mainly G8 countries also keep world agricultural prices artificially low for everyone by dumping huge quantities of food on international markets at subsidized prices. The US and European governments support their farmers through complex payments systems, and compensate them for the difference between world prices and their real production costs. In other words, they allow Northern farmers artificially to undersell producers from poor countries, with the result that the US$300 billion annual subsidies paid to Northern growers have decimated Third World peasantries.

There is no way a Mexican *campesino* can compete with huge, high-tech, subsidized US corn-growers; a Senegalese cotton or peanut farmer with Jimmy Carter's wealthy neighbours in Georgia; or Asian and Caribbean cane sugar producers with the industrialized, super-protected sugar-beet farmers of Europe. Import duties on sugar, for example, are 151 per cent in the United States, 176 per cent in Europe, 278 per cent in Japan. Such policies have obliged millions of Third World farmers to sell up and head for uncertain futures in the city, with no guarantee of alternative employment.

[114]

Relatively simple manufactures like textiles, clothing or leather goods in which poor countries could perhaps find a comparative advantage are precisely those where rich country tariffs are highest and quotas most stringent. In WTO negotiations during the 1990s, the European Union and the United States promised to remove a third of their textile quotas by 2001 and all of them by 2005. As of the beginning of the 'Doha round' of WTO negotiations in late 2002, they had removed 5 and 6 per cent respectively. Long live free trade!

The tragic destiny of raw material producers and low-end manufacturers is compounded by Third World debt and the International Monetary Fund's (IMF's) 'structural adjustment' packages that go with it. In order to qualify for loans from any source, debtor countries must follow IMF rules. The obligation to orientate their economies towards export production is at the top of the list, for this is indeed the only way they can earn hard currency for debt repayment. Dozens of debtor countries are thus producing – indeed routinely over-producing – the same narrow range of products, with the unsurprising result that prices have plummeted for all. The IMF's own figures show that, compared with 1995, producers of agricultural raw materials had, by 2003, lost a further 12 per cent of their revenues; those of metals have lost 13 per cent. World Bank figures which go back further show that since 1980 – when the debt crisis began to boil up – revenues of all non-energy commodities have been cut in half (and those of beverage producers by two-thirds). Only petroleum producers have improved their lot, mostly because they are not subject to IMF surveillance and have joined together in OPEC. Their revenues in 2003 were up by 82 per cent compared with 1995. Other producer organizations, for example the aborted coffee cartel, have failed.

Although the IMF promised the debtors a rosy future if they stuck with the austerity programme, the reality turned out to be darker. The 49 poorest countries, with 10 per cent of the world population, have seen their share of world trade drop by 40 per cent since 1980. According to the UN Conference on Trade and Development (UNCTAD), the poorest countries now account for a skeletal 0.4 per cent of global exchange. As for the whole group of so-called developing countries, UNCTAD estimates that unfair trade practices cheat them of nearly US$2 billion every day. This amounts yearly to about 14 times as much as they receive in development aid.

So 'free trade' is clearly not helping the poor as its defenders claim, and in reality is anything but 'free'. One can also argue that it's not even 'trade': not, at least, as most people would understand the word. In the twenty-first century we are no longer talking about 'England' or 'Portugal': such actors (and their national woollens or port wine firms) have been replaced in the trade game by huge transnational corporations (TNCs), headquartered overwhelmingly in the G8 countries but enjoying global reach.

At least a third of so-called world trade (over 40 per cent for the United States) is effectively not 'trade' but intra-firm exchange – for example a Ford or IBM factory receiving components from Ford and IBM factories elsewhere, then shipping finished products to yet other Ford or IBM subsidiaries. A further third of world trade takes place between different transnationals. These behemoths dwarf the trade share of local or national firms to the point where the top 500 TNCs now account for nearly 70 per cent of world trade.

Faced with such facts, the obvious questions are, 'Who does all this benefit? Why do countries sign agreements so manifestly contrary to their interests? What exactly is going on?' It seems obvious that present trade rules benefit the largest firms and the richest countries. Constantly diminishing commodity prices, for example, are godsends for huge food corporations like Nestlé or Unilever. Now, however, new twists have been added.

Until a decade ago, only manufactured goods were subject to trade negotiations, under the auspices of the General Agreement on Tariffs and Trade (GATT), founded in 1947 to reduce tariffs through a series of negotiating cycles or 'rounds'. The last of these, the 'Uruguay round', was different. Businesses in sectors other than manufactures were clamouring for trade rules to facilitate their access to foreign markets. Service providers, covering activities from accounting to construction to insurance to health and education, were among them. 'Intellectual property' companies in fields like biotechnology, software, pharmaceuticals or movies were also anxious to compete worldwide and wanted trade agreements tailored to their needs.

Negotiators during the Uruguay round, which lasted from 1986 to 1994, provided the rules they wanted. The outcome of these long years of talks was the birth of the WTO on 1 January 1995. It was no longer just a shop to talk down tariffs on manufactured goods, but became the overseer of a series of richly detailed agreements concerning, among other areas, services, agriculture, intellectual property, as well as some apparently technical but actually political questions like technical barriers to trade, or sanitary and phyto-sanitary measures. The negotiators' crowning achievement was the all-important Dispute Resolution Body (DRB), a kind of supreme court giving the WTO real teeth. Over two dozen agreements in all made up the founding text of the WTO: some 600 pages for the main agreements, with over 20,000 pages of annexes. Parliaments ratified the document usually without knowing what was in it, and less developed countries were satisfied because they had been promised 'special and differential treatment'.

However, and unsurprisingly, these agreements profited exactly those firms that had asked for them to begin with. The

European Commission website announced with disarming frankness that the General Agreement on Trade in Services (GATS) was 'first and foremost an instrument for the benefit of business'. The former Director of Services at the WTO told an audience of bankers that 'without the enormous pressures exerted by the US financial sector, particularly companies like American Express and Citicorp, there would have been no GATS and therefore perhaps no Uruguay Round and no WTO'.[1]

The intellectual property text (TRIPS) extended patent protection for TNCs from seven or eight years in most developing countries to 20 years worldwide. Under such protection, it was suddenly against WTO law for anyone but the patent owners to manufacture, say, generic drugs before the end of the patent's two-decade life. Transfers of technology were virtually halted.

The Agreement on Agriculture shuffled rich-country subsidies about among 'boxes', figuratively coloured green, blue or amber according to how damaging they were supposed to be to other countries' interests, but no firm rules for getting rid of subsidies were set. Furthermore, poor countries had to sign up for importing 5 per cent of each kind of foodstuff consumed by their people, *even if the country was self-sufficient in that product*, for example in wheat, corn or rice. This rule provided yet another opening for capital-intensive farmers to undersell and ruin local producers.

If the WTO is such a nefarious, one-sided organization, why did these countries sign on? The answer seems to be that not signing struck them as an even worse option. They believed the North's promises, they thought they would gain new market opportunities, and they were not necessarily aware of all the implications of membership, at least if we are to believe one of the first Directors of the WTO, Renato Ruggiero. In 1998, he admitted that '[various aspects] extend the reach of the Agreement into areas never before recognised as trade policy. I suspect that neither governments nor industries have yet appreciated the full scope ... the full value of existing commitments.'[2] As of the time of writing, 147 countries have become WTO members, with a few new ones joining every year, most spectacularly China in 2002. Russia and Saudi Arabia are among the major holdouts.

The disadvantages of membership are not confined to the South and are costly for ordinary people in the North as well. In the industrialized countries, we stand to lose most from forcibly lowered ecological standards and delocalization of production to cheap labour countries, particularly China. GATS is also eminently dangerous, including as it does all public services except for the police, the army and the judiciary. With twelve main sectors, including health, education, culture, the environment, tourism, energy, transport, and more than 160 subsectors, GATS covers virtually all human activities with the possible exception of religion.

This agreement changes fundamentally the notion of 'trade' regulations, which most people would conceive as stopping at the borders of a given country, dealing with goods at entry point. No longer. 'Trade' law now allows outside interference in the internal affairs of a nation. The WTO tribunal has the right to determine which national qualifications requirements and technical or health standards are 'necessary' and which are actually disguised trade barriers. Its decisions apply to local, regional and national governments, and non-compliance means sanctions will be applied against the country's products. GATS is likely to lead to legal attacks on subsidies (for example those granted to public transport or utilities); it will heighten private competition with public schools and health care facilities, and in time it will open government procurement in service areas to foreign firms.

Every time the DRB has judged a case with ecological implications, the environment has lost. If a government wants to defend public health by refusing to import a given product, it must prove beyond a scientific doubt that the product is harmful, whereas the exporter is under no obligation to prove it is innocuous. Because human biology is not as straightforward a science as, say, physics or astronomy, this requirement has proved detrimental to protection of life and health.

In a well-known case, the DRB determined that the European Union had no right to ban hormone-treated beef because it had not proved it was dangerous to health. When, in deference to hugely negative public opinion, the European Union stuck to its refusal, the DRB authorized the United States and Canada to apply sanctions on European products of their choice. That is how a sheep farmer and Roquefort cheese producer called José Bové became an international celebrity after he and his friends dismantled a McDonald's. The farmers were making a serious point. They had nothing to do with the beef hormone case in question, they had committed no crime and broken no rules, yet they could get no redress from any elected body or from the EU Commission. In the Larzac, a poor and barren area of France, they also had no alternatives to sheep farming and Roquefort production. Their cheese was chosen arbitrarily – along with Danish hams, Italian truffles and various other European products – for sanctions, causing huge marketing losses and a sudden collapse of their livelihoods. What kind of judicial system punishes innocent people simply because their government was trying to protect public health?

The DRB is able to invoke other 'legal principles' peculiar to the WTO, which most civilized people would reject. For instance, according to WTO rules, a football made by children working 14 hours a day is 'the same' as one made under decent conditions by unionized labour. It is WTO-illegal to invoke a given product's history, or in the jargon, its 'processes and methods of production', because one must not discriminate between 'like' products. The only exception the DRB has made to this rule so far was to accept, on appeal, that asbestos can be banned because it indisputably causes cancer, even though the first DRB hearing determined that it was 'like' glass fibre or other insulation materials.

What can anyone, in North or South, do about an organization so totally biased in favour of giant corporations and against the needs of citizens or ecological protection? At the beginning, the answer seemed to be 'nothing'. Few people or non-governmental organizations (NGOs) were paying attention during the Uruguay round when the WTO was conceived and born, and the whole process, insofar as it was known at all, seemed unutterably technical and boring. How wrong we were! As we discovered too late, it's easier to prevent something that does not yet exist than to get rid of an institution when it has become part of the official landscape. Furthermore, although it brags about being a 'one-country-one-vote' organization and claims decisions are made by consensus, the WTO is unaccountable and undemocratic, if by 'democratic' one means that public opinion can influence it in any way.

For activists, only two avenues are left open: shut down the WTO physically or influence its member states. The first of these avenues was hugely successful in Seattle at the ministerial meeting of November 1999. Innovative, mostly American NGOs combined creative non-violence with individual courage and inventiveness to stop the negotiations.[3] But they were soon up and running again, and two years later, at the Doha (Qatar) ministerial meeting where few foreigners could hope to be present, a whole new round was launched. Then in September 2003, coalitions of like-minded Third World governments took up the struggle in Cancun, Mexico and stopped negotiations in their tracks by refusing to move if the North insisted on maintaining agricultural subsidies. They also refused the US–European attempt to put even more subjects on the table.[4] A few months later, however, in July 2004, these same countries agreed to restart negotiations on the basis of a vague declaration announcing that subsidies would be dealt with (no calendar or figures attached) and that the new subjects would be off-limits at least until the end of this round.

The strategy of trying to block negotiations, in the street or at the bargaining table, has severe limitations. The process may be down for a while, but it is never out. The other strategy is a popular revolt to influence member governments. Some NGOs, for example ATTAC-France, have orchestrated this strategy in an anti-GATS campaign. Starting from the principle that the WTO is undemocratic and cannot be changed directly, and that the European Trade Commissioner who negotiates for all 25 EU members is not accountable except to member states, the only remaining strategy to force change is to make one's own government insist on it. And the quickest way to force a government to change its policies is through elected representatives at all levels of responsibility. The GATS campaign therefore calls on municipal, departmental and regional councils to declare themselves GATS-free zones and demand a moratorium on negotiations and a new mandate for the European Trade Commissioner. The movement's ultimate aim is of course to remove health, education, the environment, culture, water and all public services from the remit of the agreement. At the end of 2004, over 620 French '*collectivités*' (local governments) covering well over two-thirds of the French population, had voted such official resolutions. In mid-November many of them met in 'Estates General' to plan further common action. The steering committee made up of local elected officials from different levels of government and political parties has presented the Estates General's demands formally to the president and prime minister. The movements ambition is to hold Europe-wide 'Estates General' in 2005. Many other NGOs, including ATTACs in several European countries, are joining in the campaign.

Although we have no guarantee of winning, we do know that 'free trade' is the freedom of the fox in the henhouse. Citizens' movements throughout the world, especially in the G8 countries, should join in repudiating an organization that exists by and for transnational corporations and is hell-bent on enforcing the 'race to the bottom'. As all countries try to win by increasing the repression of labour and accelerate the destruction of the planet, as governments turn more and more activities over to the private sector; inequality, poverty and democratic regression will be the only outcomes. World trade requires rules, yes, but not these rules. The WTO must go back to the drawing board and next time, citizens must be present and be heard.

NOTES

1 Hartridge, David (1997) 'What the General Agreement on Trade in Services can do', symposium held by the international law firm Clifford Change on 'Opening markets for banking worldwide': see <http://cliffordchance.com>.

2 Ruggiero was referring specifically to GATS but his remarks could apply to many other WTO agreements.

3 For a riveting fictional yet true account of Seattle, read Robert Newman's splendid new novel, *The Fountain at the Centre of the World* (Verso, 2004).

4 These subjects, known collectively as the Singapore Issues (from the place they were first proposed in 1996) were investment, government procurement, competition policy and trade facilitation.

9 Food security

Caroline Lucas and Michael Woodin

> If you are looking for a way to get people to lean on you
> and be dependent on you, in terms of their co-operating
> with you, it seems to me that food-dependence would be
> terrific.
>
> US Vice President Hubert Humphrey[1]

Agriculture is in crisis. In both the developed and developing worlds, farmers are losing their livelihoods, and monocultures are suffocating the rich intricacies of the rural economy, as well as causing massive soil erosion, destroying natural habitats and reducing biodiversity. In an era when more than enough food is produced to feed the world, millions go hungry. At the time of writing, the World Food Programme estimated that 40 million people in Africa were in urgent need of food aid.[2] Half of India's population is malnourished.[3] Even in a prosperous country like the United Kingdom, 7 per cent of the population – four million people – live in food poverty.[4]

The response of the world's largest economic powers is starkly hypocritical. The G8, particularly the United States and the European Union countries, maintain massive agricultural subsidies at home, yet demand the liberalization of agriculture abroad. In April 2002, President George W Bush put his name to a US$248.6 billion farm bill that will raise US agricultural subsidies by up to 80 per cent a year for the next ten years.[5] Surpluses, generated in part by EU Common Agricultural Policy (CAP) production subsidies, are dumped at artificially low prices on newly liberalized markets in developing countries, with devastating effects.

The liberalization of agriculture that the G8 is attempting to foist on the developing world is a very large part of the problem; the solution is to be found in achieving the goal of food security through the localization of agriculture.

FROM FOOD SECURITY TO INTERNATIONAL COMPETITIVENESS

Ironically, the main motivation for the North's creation of its extensive systems of agricultural subsidies was to achieve domestic food security. The CAP is a typical example. Its objectives were defined in 1957 in response to the widespread food shortages Europe was experiencing at the time. They were to increase productivity, boost farmers' incomes, stabilize markets, and crucially, to ensure an adequate supply of reasonably priced food. Understandably, these were popular objectives at the time, and a complex range of mechanisms was instituted to implement them. These included production subsidies, direct payments to producers to guarantee minimum prices, levies on imports, export subsidies, and market intervention to purchase surplus production.

However, it is now widely accepted that the CAP has dramatically overachieved at least some of its objectives, so much so that it is now generating huge surpluses, which are dumped on world markets at prices that undercut local produce. For example, the European dairy giant Arla Foods exports around £43 million worth of dairy produce to the Dominican Republic, for which it receives £11 million in export subsidies from the European Union. This makes Arla's milk 25 per cent cheaper than local produce. It is no surprise, then, that over the last 20 years 10,000 Dominican Republic dairy farmers have lost their jobs.[6]

Rapid intensification of EU agriculture has also led to larger field sizes, increased mechanization and heavier use of chemical and energy inputs. Hedgerows have been grubbed out, ponds drained, soils eroded and water resources polluted. Populations of birds, mammals and insects have declined dramatically.

Having more than achieved food security for itself, the G8 turned its attentions to the South, seeking new markets for its surplus products. But it is not just dumped exports from the North that are distorting markets for agricultural goods in the South. The twin forces of the World Trade Organization's (WTO's) Agreement on Agriculture (AOA) and the structural adjustment policies of the International Monetary Fund (IMF) are also forcing developing countries, often against their better judgement, to gear production to the export market. Already volatile markets for cash crops have been flooded as more countries are forced to export the same range of basic commodities, and the prices farmers receive for their produce have collapsed as a result.

For example, in the mid-1990s the IMF bulldozed Haiti into liberalizing its rice markets. As a result, it was flooded with cheap US imports and local production collapsed, destroying tens of thousands of rural livelihoods. A decade ago Haiti was self-sufficient in rice; today it spends half of its export earnings importing rice from the United States. In many of the least developed countries, the loss of export earnings attributable to the distorting effects of EU and US subsidies far outweighs the savings made through debt relief.[7]

The shift in emphasis from overcoming post-war food shortages to prising open new markets for subsidized exports amounts to a dramatic change in policy. Countries are now being forced to compete to produce each other's food as cheaply as possible, and at the expense of domestic production. Local food security is being swapped for mandatory trade rules that are biased toward agribusiness, industrial production and long-distance transport. Recently, the UK Food and Farming minister, Larry Whitty, provided a blunt summary of this policy, when he said, 'a [self sufficiency] target is not what drives policy. Being competitive drives policy.'[8]

THE GREAT FOOD SWAP

Unsurprisingly, this policy shift has produced a dramatic increase in the international food trade. Over the last 30 years for example, exports of a variety of food products from EU member states increased by between 164 per cent and 1340 per cent. However, it is not as if the EU has achieved self-sufficiency and is exporting its surplus – it remains one of the world's largest food importers. Over exactly the same period, food imports into the European Union increased, in some cases by nearly 300 per cent. This pattern is repeated at the global level. Between 1968 and 1998 world food production increased by 84 per cent, yet over the same period international trade in food products almost trebled, with trade flows doubling for almost every food category.[9]

Of course, conventional economists would welcome this as evidence of increasing specialization in food production, such that countries are concentrating on producing those products for which they have a comparative advantage and are importing foods that are produced more efficiently elsewhere. However, closer inspection of the figures reveals that a large part of the growth in international trade in food is accounted for by simultaneous imports and exports of the same products between exactly the same countries. The United Kingdom and the European Union provide telling case studies. In 1998 Britain imported 61,400 tonnes of poultry meat from the Netherlands and exported 33,100 tonnes of poultry meat to the Netherlands. In the same year it imported 240,000 tonnes of pork and 125,000 tonnes of lamb, while it exported 195,000 tonnes of pork and 102,000 tonnes of lamb. In 1997, the United Kingdom imported 126 million litres of milk and exported 270 million litres of milk. In the same year 23,000 tonnes of milk powder were imported into the United Kingdom and 153,000 tonnes were exported. In 1999, the European Union imported 44,000 tonnes of meat from Argentina, 11,000 tonnes from Botswana, 40,000 tonnes from Poland and over 70,000 tonnes from Brazil. In the same year the meat exports from the European Union to the rest of the world totalled 874,211 tonnes.[10]

Increasingly, agriculture is held in thrall to the overwhelming and hugely mistaken imperative of international competitiveness. Producers are being locked into an absurd and wasteful global food swap, and everyone, save a few agribusiness giants, is paying the price.

PAYING FOR THE GREAT FOOD SWAP

Food security, hunger and development

In the developed world, the erosion of localized patterns of production and consumption has a serious impact on the environment and the health of rural economies, but in much of the developing world the loss of local food security is also a matter of life or death. This was tragically illustrated at the WTO

Ministerial Meeting in Cancun in September 2003, when South Korean farmer Lee Kyoung-Hae committed suicide during a farmer's march in protest at WTO policies. An insight into what drove Lee to take his own life can be found in an article he wrote the month before for the *Korean Agrofood* magazine:

> Soon after the Uruguay Round of the GATT (now the WTO) was signed in 1992 (opening Korean markets to rich countries and allowing the dumping of rice and other foods) we farmers realised that our destinies were out of our hands. We could do nothing but watch our lovely rural communities being destroyed.... It is a fact that since the WTO agreement, we have never been paid our production costs. Sometimes prices dropped to a quarter of what they used to be.... Once I ran to a house where a farmer abandoned his life by drinking a toxic chemical because of his uncontrollable debts. I could do nothing but listen to the howling of his wife.

He concludes:

> My warning goes to all citizens that uncontrolled multi-national corporations and a small number of big WTO members' officials are leading to an undesirable globalisation of inhumane, environment-distorting, farmer-killing and undemocratic [policies]. It should be stopped immediately, otherwise the false logic of neo-liberalism will perish the diversity of global agriculture and bring disaster to all.

Current estimates suggest 40 million people in Africa are in need of food aid, a situation that has been made far worse by the globalization of agriculture. Malawi would have had sufficient grain supplies to get through the drought in 2004 had it not been pressurized into selling its surplus by the World Bank. Farmers in many southern African states have been forced by their governments to give up cultivating everything apart from maize, which can be exported and is very productive in a good year, even though traditional crops such as sorghum and millet are much better at coping with fluctuations in moisture and would have provided some protection from the drought. And the shocking fact is that in the famine of the 1980s, Ethiopia was a net exporter of grain, and nearly 80 per cent of malnourished children in the South live in countries that have food surpluses.[11] In Zimbabwe and Tanzania farmers are even compelled to buy seed from authorized companies, which only supply maize. Increasingly, these companies are being taken over by predominantly US-based agribusiness transnational corporations (TNCs), further undermining local food security.[12]

The policies of the G8, whether through the WTO, World Bank or IMF, are working in the wrong direction. They are enslaving developing countries to volatile international markets for monoculture cash crops, thus destroying their ability to provide for local need. Even bilateral food aid tends to undermine local production. In times of food emergency it would be better if food were bought as locally as possible, thus sustaining any remaining local production.

Increased international trade is not the answer to food poverty. Where hunger exists, what is often lacking is not food, but access to either the money to buy it or the land on which to grow it.[13] In some poorer countries where millions are landless and hungry this situation is compounded by the large-scale cultivation of cattle feed for export. It is estimated for example that for every acre farmed in the United Kingdom, two more are farmed overseas in order to meet the feed requirements of our intensively farmed livestock. Imported feed, such as cassava, soya beans and soya cake, makes up about 30 per cent of all European animal feed. An estimated 5.6 million acres in Brazil and around 1.2 million acres in Argentina are devoted to soya bean production for export – land that would be better used by local people to grow food for local need.

Small farms under threat

The intensification of agriculture has caused massive job losses in the sector. In the United Kingdom, the total agricultural labour force has declined by 20 per cent over the past 20 years; it fell by nearly 20,000 people in 1999 alone.[14] The UK Policy Commission on Food and Farming reported that 51,300 farmers and farm workers left the industry in the two years to June 2000, equivalent to 70 a day. These job losses are often associated with farm amalgamations, and UK ministers expect that by 2005 as many as 25 per cent of farms – almost all small ones – will have closed or merged, with 50,000 people forced to leave the industry.[15]

As workers leave the countryside, so other support services decline. By the end of the 1990s, rural decline in the United Kingdom had become acute: 42 per cent of rural parishes had no shop, 43 per cent had no post office, 83 per cent had no doctor, 49 per cent had no school and 75 per cent had no daily bus service.[16]

The loss of agricultural employment is paralleled throughout the developed world. Canada lost three-quarters of its farmers between 1941 and 1996. In the United States there were 6.8 million farmers in 1935; today there are fewer than 1.9 million – less than the US prison population.[17] In the European Union at least 500,000 farm jobs are lost each year. With the enlargement of the European Union to include countries like Poland where farming still accounts for more than 27 per cent of the workforce, this situation is likely to get worse.

The developed world's experience is a foretaste of what is likely to happen in developing countries as their agriculture systems are increasingly 'liberalized' under policies promoted by the G8. Already, between 1985 and 1995 in Brazil, 5 million farmers left the land.[18] The Indian state of Andhra Pradesh has adopted a development policy 'Vision 2020' that aims to achieve developed nation status by 2020. Under the plans, small landholdings are to be amalgamated and farmed under contract to major agribusiness companies. Intensive plantation-style production for the commercial seed and export markets, much of it using GM crops, is to replace small-scale family-based farming, with the loss of an estimated 20 million rural livelihoods.[19] Similarly in China, rapid urbanization is placing 400 million rural livelihoods at risk.

The decline in rural employment on smaller farms is no accidental by-product of the globalization of agriculture; it is a deliberate feature of G8 governments' policies around the world. The same employment-destroying policies are being exported around the world. Andhra Pradesh's Vision 2020 polices have received backing from the World Bank and the UK's Department for International Development (DFID). Indeed, the Government of Andhra Pradesh receives two-thirds of DFID's entire aid budget to India, despite evidence of unease in the department about the Vision 2020 programme. An internal DFID memo reportedly states that Vision 2020 has 'major failings' and 'says nothing substantial about the implied need to provide alternative agricultural income … to those who would be displaced from agriculture by [land] consolidation'. The memo concludes, 'The promotion of contract farming … has many negative implications for the food security and wider livelihood security of the poor.'[20]

LOCAL FOOD – GLOBAL SOLUTION

It is clear, then, that the policies of the G8 are reducing food security in the South, and that we urgently need alternative models. Many farmers and citizens groups in both North and South are now coming to the conclusion that local food security must replace international competitiveness as the central goal of agricultural policy. It may be an unfashionable and undervalued concept, but local food security is the only way to feed the world without incurring the hidden costs of intensive agriculture. Countries (or geographically and economically cohesive regions) should have the right to determine their own policies on food security: in short, they should enjoy 'food sovereignty'.

To achieve this, we will need a fundamental shift in the balance of power over agricultural policy away from the agribusiness and supermarket TNCs, as well as a fundamental revision of the rules of the WTO and the other free trade treaties to enable the reintroduction of protective safeguards for domestic economies, including tariffs and quotas.

A rather predictable objection to the proposal to allow import controls is that they would be unfair to poor producers in the South whose livelihoods depend upon access to Northern markets. This would be a fair criticism if the only element of these proposals were the erection of import barriers in the North. However, they also include measures that would end the dumping of the North's subsidized exports in the South, and uphold the right of developing countries to impose barriers against imports that would otherwise undermine their own food security – the so-called 'development box' proposal. For this reason, farmers and activists in the South are already advocating proposals very similar to these.

For example, Indian academics and activists are calling for the reintroduction of import controls as a response to the collapse in rural incomes following a WTO ruling on Quantitative Restrictions, brought by the United States, that enforced import liberalization. A recent report by the prestigious Delhi-based Centre for the Study of Global Trade Systems and Development identified the importing of foreign goods and services without quantitative or tariff restrictions as instrumental in destroying India's agriculture and industry, and in causing further unemployment. It called for more emphasis on domestic investment, and the protection of domestic employment through the curbing of foreign investment, selective capital controls and higher tariffs.[21] The Indian People's Movement Against the WTO, made up of trade unions, farmers' organizations and other activists, echoes these demands.[22]

Indeed, many prominent commentators in the developing world are also highly critical of the emphasis on agricultural exports as a strategy for poverty reduction. The Indian academic and activist Vandana Shiva has said:

> The ecological and democratic model of food security is based as far as possible on ecological production and local consumption. Trade liberalisation ignores this truth.... Diverting food from rural households and communities to global markets or diverting land from food crops for local consumption to luxury crops for export to the rich North might show growth in dollars in international trade figures but it translates into increased hunger and deprivation in the rural areas of the Third World.[23]

By the same argument, hunger and deprivation will be reduced in Southern countries once they are freed to divert food and land back from the global export markets to their rural households and communities.

Crucially, these trade-related measures are part of the wider localization agenda that involves many other initiatives to complement the global shift towards local food security. One such initiative is the cancellation of debts. This would remove the chief factors that are forcing developing countries into dependence on export markets in the first place. Nevertheless, to give time for producers, both Northern and Southern, to adapt, the proposals should be introduced gradually and with, if necessary, as much effort expended to achieve international consensus as is currently employed to achieve further trade liberalization.

In the South, as in the North, food security is best delivered through simple, locally based solutions. Radical land reform policies that give landless peasants access to small areas of land will do far more to alleviate hunger than forcing small farmers off the land or into dependence on agribusiness companies and export monoculture. Even in situations of acute hunger, simple improvements to the local food distribution and storage systems are often all that is required to ensure that everyone has adequate access to food. In Zambia there are large surpluses of cassava in the north of the country, but it cannot be moved to the hungry south. A similar situation prevails in Ethiopia.

The 'best' efforts of the international institutions, and the policies of the G8, have done little to solve the problem of hunger over the last few decades. In fact, their export-oriented solutions have proved to be an integral part of the problem. They should adopt instead the global solution of local food security.

NOTES

1   Quoted in Goldsmith, E (2001) 'Development as colonialism', in E Goldsmith and G Mander (eds), *The Case Against the Global Economy and for a Turn Towards Localization*, Earthscan, London.

2   Carroll, R (2003) '40 million starving "as world watches Iraq"', *Guardian,* 9 April.

3   Food and Agriculture Organization (FAO) (2003) *World Agriculture 2003: Main findings*, FAO, Rome.
4   Gordon, D et al. (2000) *Poverty and Social Exclusion in Britain*, Joseph Rowntree Foundation/York Publishing Services, York.
5   Watkins, K (2002) 'Greed in action: US farming subsidies will hit world's poor', *Guardian Society*, 5 June.
6   Oxfam (2002) *Milking the CAP: How Europe's dairy regime is devastating livelihoods in the developing world*, Oxfam Briefing Paper no. 34, Oxfam, Oxford.
7   Watkins (2002) (see note 5).
8   Lord Whitty, speaking at the Royal Smithfield Show, 25 November 2002.
9   This data is drawn from FAO (2001), *Food Balance Sheet Database*, FAO, Rome. Fuller details and analysis can be found in Lucas, C (2001) *Swapping the Great Food Swap: Relocalising Europe's food supply*, Greens/European Free Alliance in the European Parliament, Brussels, <http://www.carolinelucasmep.org.uk/publications/greatfoodswap.html>.
10   Ibid.
11   Meadows, D (2000) 'Can organic farming feed the world?' *Organic Farming Magazine*, USA, May.
12   Egziabher, T B G (2003) 'How (not) to feed Africa', *New Internationalist*, no 353, pp 14–15.
13   FAO (2000) *The State of Food Insecurity in the World*, FAO, Rome.
14   Ministry of Agriculture, Fisheries and Food UK (MAFF) (2000) *Agriculture in the UK, 1999*, MAFF, London.
15   Wintour, P (2001) 'Extent of farm crisis revealed', *Guardian*, 11 April.
16   Countryside Agency (1999) *The State of the Countryside: Summary of key facts*, Countryside Agency, Cheltenham.
17   Ainger, K (2003) 'The new peasants' revolt', *New Internationalist*, no 353, pp 9–13.
18   Ibid.
19   Ainger, K (2003) 'The market and the monsoon', *New Internationalist*, no 353, pp 22–27.
20   Quoted in Ainger (as note 19).
21   Ghosh, A (2001) *Economic Reforms in India: A critical assessment*, Centre for the Study of Global Trade Systems and Development, New Delhi.

22 See
    <http://www.mindfully.org/WTO/Indian-WBJA-Against-WTO.htm>.
23 Vandana Shiva, quoted in Hines, C (2000) *Localization: A global
    manifesto*, Earthscan, London, p 207.

10 'War on terror'
on racism, asylum and immigration

Salma Yaqoob

RACISM IS CENTRAL TO THE NEO-LIBERAL OFFENSIVE

The wonderful worldwide demonstrations on 15 February 2003 saw millions stand together in opposition to war. That day gave us a glimpse of what another world would be like: a world united against war and oppression but diverse in its culture, faith, colour and race. This outpouring of solidarity spoke of the deep desire of the majority of humanity to express what we have in common and to resist those who wish to set us against each other. Such an enriching and powerful experience was a powerful antidote to the thesis of a 'clash of civilizations', and a rejection of the racism that is increasingly a feature of world and European politics.

Despite its barbarism, war cannot be seen as some form of accidental irrationality. It is, in the well-worn phrase from Clausewitz, 'the continuation of politics by other means'. Imperialist war today is not a regrettable interlude on an uninterrupted path towards peace and prosperity. It is the sharpest expression of the imposition of neo-liberal policies on an increasingly divided world. And woven into every aspect of this neo-liberal offensive is the ideology of racism. If we genuinely want to create a 'different world', we must understand the significance of this racist ideology and the particular shape it takes today.

CAUSES OF MIGRATION: ESCAPING POVERTY AND WAR

Today the governments of rich countries want to stop people from entering their countries, and are imposing strict immigration controls. However, while loudly decrying the dangers of immigrants and asylum seekers, these governments do not own up to their role in forcing people to leave their home countries in the first place. People need to migrate mainly for two reasons: first to escape poverty to improve their economic situation, and second to escape from wars and persecution. Neo-liberal economic policies and imperialist wars on the part of rich countries have a direct hand in both these causes of forced migration.

While poorer countries are condemned for their inefficiencies and lack of 'development' in relation to the West (reinforcing the myth of the inferior ability of non-whites to 'progress'), the truth is that the economic policies of richer countries have imposed greater and greater poverty on the Third World. The result is an extreme polarization of wealth internationally.

The World Trade Organization (WTO), International Monetary Fund (IMF) and World Bank reinforce the industrial domination of major capitalist powers. Poorer countries are prevented from protecting their own industries and agriculture while the rich demand access to their markets and resources. Dependence on international finance is used to impose neo-liberal 'shock therapy', with privatizations and cuts to welfare provisions made a condition of further aid. And through the debt system the richest countries of the world extract far more from the poor than is returned to them in aid. The results have been catastrophic, and many countries have discovered that the neo-liberal medicine they have been prescribed is in reality a poisoned chalice.

Millions have been denied the resources of their own country, denied food subsidies, health and education services, and pauperized by the 'fixed market' that goes by the name of the 'free market'. As Mike Davis notes, 'Much of the urban world … is rushing backwards to the age of Dickens.' Unable to compete with Western agribusiness, millions have moved from rural areas to cities in search of a job in order to survive. This migration has led to over 900 million people – a staggering 78.2 per cent of the urban population of the least developed countries and fully a third of the global urban population – to live in slums in abject poverty.[1] It is this poverty that provides the impetus for a small proportion of these people to migrate further to other countries.

Such migration can be the difference between life and death. Migrants frequently work to support families at home. And this income comes without the strings attached to foreign aid. At the end of the 1980s, the World Bank estimated that US$65 billion in earnings by foreign workers went back to their countries of origin – about US$20 billion more than the sum of aid from wealthier to poorer countries.[2]

Some refugee crises are triggered by direct Western military interventions, as in Afghanistan. People flee their homes to escape bombing. Other movements of people are triggered by local conflicts and repression. These are often rooted in the West's support for elites in these countries, who benefit from allowing Western exploitation of their countries. Poverty and war go hand in hand. And this generalized social catastrophe is compelling millions of people to leave their homes in the hope of survival.

THE MAJORITY OF MIGRANTS REMAIN IN THE SOUTH

In recent years international migration has ignited a large debate in the so-called receiving countries, where it is assumed that migrants benefit materially at the expense of receiver communities. The truth is that the overwhelming majority of forced migrants remain in the South, often in poor areas bordering their place of origin. It is the South that carries the burden of a global refugee population, Pakistan and Iran alone host almost one-third of the world's 12 million refugees.[3]

Most migration experts acknowledge that the relatively few who do come to the North cannot be seen as a serious strain for rich countries. Indeed there is a growing realization that immigration is necessary for the North –for both demographic[4] and economic reasons.[5]

BENEFITS OF MIGRANTS TO THE NORTH

As Western populations age, so the need for migrant labour increases. 'Very strong volumes of migration would be needed',[6] the Organisation for Economic Co-operation and Development (OECD) concluded in 1998, 'to change the trend in ageing populations' in wealthy economies. According to a British Home Office study published in 1999, existing migrants contributed £2.6 billion more in taxes than they received in benefits and services like health and education.[7]

Those who talk of migrants as burdens rarely acknowledge the fact that since they tend to be a self-selected group of young, fit adults, rich countries benefit from their labour without having contributed to their education and health costs. Furthermore, migrants typically do many of the '3D' – dirty, dangerous and difficult jobs – which are increasingly rejected by national workers. This suits employers, who are able to keep wages lower and have access to a temporary workforce, which is less demanding than the core of permanent workers.

EXPLOITATION OF MIGRANTS

Despite the official hostility to migrants, the G8 leaders nonetheless have to balance the political benefits of attacking migrants with the real economic benefits these workers may bring. Needless to say, the form in which this is done aims at the super-exploitation of this group of workers.

In an initiative that combines 'sublime cynicism with ruthless political calculation',[8] George W Bush and his neoconservative friends have set the tone in a new plan for the millions of Mexican and Central American immigrant workers in the United States. Bush has proposed giving temporary residence to illegal workers:

> In effect this legalises a sub-caste of low-wage labour without providing a mechanism for the estimated 5 to 7 million undocumented workers already in the US to achieve permanent residence or citizenship. Toilers without votes or permanent domicile, of course, are a Republican utopia. The Bush plan would provide Wal-Mart and McDonald's with a stable, almost infinite supply of indentured labour.[9]

It is clear that economic migration is acceptable as long as it continues to offer itself for super-exploitation.

XENOPHOBIA AND 'SECURITY' – WEAPONS OF MASS DISTRACTION

Given that economic migration has more benefits than disadvantages for the North, the heated debates in our countries around immigration controls and asylum are somewhat perplexing. The official discourse of dangers posed by immigrants and asylum seekers, however, makes sense from an ideological and political perspective.

The imperialist and neo-liberal policies of rich countries are directly responsible for the social and economic catastrophes that afflict much of the world. But these governments will not own up to their own responsibility for the crises that drive this migration. They respond instead by exploiting fear and suspicion, and erect barriers to prevent migration from South to North or from East to West. They deliberately employ xenophobia, and now increasingly 'security', as weapons of mass distraction.

The ideology of racism serves to obscure the real reasons for migration and to legitimize the immense human suffering that is imposed on the majority of humanity. As one Sri Lankan pointed out at a conference of European aid givers: 'It is your economics that makes our politics that makes us refugees in your countries. We are here because you are still there.'[10]

Right-wing nationalist parties crudely use anti-foreigner feeling to bolster support for themselves. Immigration controls were first introduced in the United Kingdom in 1905 as a result of racist agitation by the far right against Jewish refugees. The ever-tightening immigration regime has served only to feed and legitimize racism. State powers are used to reinforce rather than challenge popular racist prejudices. The following headlines from the British newspaper the *Daily Express* in 2002 give a little taste: 'Cut benefits and stem the asylum tide' (21 January); 'Refugees in under age sex scandal' (25 January); 'Got Aids? Welcome to Britain' (7 April); 'Asylum law lets perverts stay in UK' (7 July). The media, however, only take their cue from the politicians, many of whom compete to prove who is 'toughest' – further shifting the terms of debate to the far right.

The British Labour government has even sought to revise the right of refugees to seek asylum in any country, as currently embodied in the 1951 United Nations Geneva Convention. It has urged European governments to finance reception camps in countries neighbouring the refugees, from whom governments can select a favoured few for asylum in Europe. Given that the migration crisis is a 'bogus' one in the North, such measures can be seen to be particularly cruel.

More insidiously we are seeing the 'securitization'[11] of migration issues. This was underway following the end of the Cold War and the economic crises that swept Eastern Europe. Following the attacks on 11 September 2001, calls for immigration control intensified. The US elite began to link discourses on immigration with discourses on security, 'rogue states' and Islamic fundamentalism – resulting in a neo-liberal anti-immigrant onslaught.

THE 'WAR ON TERROR' AND THE NEW FORM OF RACISM

The 'war on terror' is the ideological cover for the United States to reassert its military and economic dominance on the world and to remap the Middle East in its own strategic interests. Old-fashioned imperial conquest has been repackaged and disguised as a defence of 'civilization' against 'global terror'. The 'threat of Muslim fundamentalism' is to White House propagandists today what the bogey of communism was during the Cold War. This new phase of imperialism requires a new phase of mass fear to legitimize wars abroad, and increase the powers of governments over their citizens at home. Scared citizens ask fewer questions of their governments.

Today it takes the form of Islamophobia – a fear and hatred of Muslims – who are constructed as an enemy both 'without' and 'within', ready to carry out terrorist attacks. Public opinion has been manipulated through the grossest of stereotypes and simplifications. Muslims as a whole – whether living in other nations, arriving as immigrants, or already settled in Western countries – are associated with crude caricatures of evil: such as Saddam, bin Laden, suicide bombers and evil imams. Non-Muslims are encouraged to unite against these cartoon ogres. Endless speculation around 'terror alerts' – which are usually found to have no basis – feed a generalized mood of fear and paranoia.

Anti-Muslim racism does not just stop at a hostile mindset, it is acted out at the structural and institutional as well as popular levels. In the name of security, the rule of law itself has been withdrawn from Muslims – abroad in Guantanamo and in the United Kingdom in Belmarsh Prison. The long-held principles of innocent until proven guilty and the right to transparent processes have been overturned.

Whatever the protestations of ordinary Muslims about their loyalty and peaceful nature, they are subject to police stops, to police raids, to imprisonment without charge, to the shutting-down of bank accounts, to censoring of sermons in mosques – in addition to abuse in the media, attacks from politicians and racist violence. The kind of rhetoric previously associated with far-right extremists is now acceptable in establishment discourse. The *Daily Telegraph* – traditionally the house paper of the Conservative Party – goes so far as to print articles comparing Muslims to dogs.[12] Muslims abroad live in fear of their countries being attacked, and those living in the West fear being attacked in the street and their homes – all the while being portrayed as the threat to others.

But Muslims are not just assumed to pose a physical threat to Western countries: they are also regarded as posing a cultural threat. Adherence to Islamic norms and values, it seems, threatens notions of national cohesion and even 'Europeanness' itself.

> This obsession with preserving a caricature of British identity necessarily obscures the racism and cultural supremacism that remains a part of it. Thus, it is Muslim separatism that needs to be tackled rather than British racism and the 'problem' is with the culture of particular groups rather than the racism of society. The solution, then, is to make those groups more British rather than society less racist.[13]

This has led to a wave of anti-Islamic racism at the same time as great emphasis on a national identity that eschews pluralism and diversity. There is now a deliberate shift towards monoculturalism in Western countries. This ideological offensive serves to give a sense of unified purpose and identity to citizens of nations who in reality have different interests. It diverts attention from the growing inequalities that neo-liberalism has brought about even in the developed countries themselves – as well as between North and South.

It is therefore no accident that a debate on national identity is taking place across Europe which has the problematization of Muslims at its heart. Any notion of Islam other than an extreme one is never considered, and the idea that for many Muslims their faith confirms for them the equality of all human beings and motivates them to seek the betterment of the whole of society is beyond comprehension.

Each nation is using arguments consistent with its historical character, but the anti-Muslim theme is consistent.[14] In the United Kingdom, the theme has been 'community cohesion' following urban riots in northern England in the summer of 2001. In the Netherlands a cross-party parliamentary report published in January 2004 concluded that Muslims had failed to integrate and that ethnic ghettos were tearing the country apart: the solution was Muslims 'becoming Dutch'. In Germany the national identity debates have centred on the superiority of '*Leitkultur*' (leading culture) over immigrant (Muslim) cultures. In Denmark the focus has been on the 'intolerant culture' amongst immigrants that prevents integration. In France the principle of *laicité* (state secularism) has underpinned the noisy debate around the issue of Muslim girls wearing the hijab (headscarf) to school. The French president described the wearing of hijab as 'a sort of aggression and a symbol of anti-Western sentiment'.[15]

While emphasizing the lack of Muslim integration, the debate has also applied similar rhetoric to asylum seekers, often using the terms 'Muslim', 'immigrant' and 'asylum seeker' interchangeably, reinforcing the idea of Muslims as the foreign 'other' – even if communities have been settled for generations.

The idea of 'us' and 'them' is constantly evoked in these debates. The racism is increasingly blatant. Daniel Pipes – a journalist nominated by President Bush to the board of United States Institute of Peace – spoke of immigrant Muslims in western Europe as 'brown-skinned peoples cooking strange foods and maintaining different standards of hygiene. Muslim customs are more troublesome than most.'[16]

INTERWEAVING OF SECURITY RISKS AND RESPONSES

In the post-9/11 context many countries have placed themselves on what is virtually a 'national emergency' footing. New measures and institutions tend to function according to the logic of 'security' rather than the principles of the rule of law. The range of situations in which force has been legitimized has been substantially extended.

The same neo-liberal logic that justifies military interventions against 'rogue states' is also applied to interventions against asylum seekers, Muslim communities, and even to anti-government protestors. All these differing issues are now treated as security threats, and the same agencies are employed to deal with them: security firms, intelligence services, customs, police and prison services. Under the guise of the 'war on terror' the distinctions between these issues have been wilfully blurred. In this way, seeking asylum, belonging to the Muslim community and participating in protests, while perfectly lawful, are now being treated as security risks – the same as acts of terrorism, organized crime and handling drugs. The employment of the security logic has thus led to a criminalization not just of Muslims (who can be detained without charge) and asylum seekers (who are increasingly being placed in detention centres) but of virtually anyone who challenges the government. The fear around security threats has helped pave the way for more autocratic governments.

The proposal to establish a common border police force to carry out surveillance work, investigate crime and conduct customs controls at the European Union's external borders, as well as fighting terrorism, illegal immigration and trafficking, is a powerful indicator of how these different issues are being interwoven.[17] Post-9/11 the 'war on terror' has provided an excuse for increasing constraints on the movement of refugees and economic migrants, as well as curtailing their human rights. Security considerations have provided both the justification and the opportunity for strengthening the boundaries between the global North and the global South.

ANOTHER WORLD IS POSSIBLE

This new phase of racism obscures what is really responsible for the global economic and social crisis. It is used to shore up political support in the West for military adventures. It diverts attention from the real attacks on working people in the West itself. And it serves to criminalize resistance at home and abroad.

Our campaigns are many and varied. Our movements struggle against war, the debt burden, repression and attacks on civil liberties. We campaign against the arms trade, we oppose attacks on asylum seekers, and we reject Islamophobia. At first glance they are all distinct issues. But they are all linked by the centrality of racism to imperialism and the unjust economics of neo-liberalism.

The leaders of the G8 represent the pinnacle of the world system that generates such oppression and reaction. No concession can be given to the racist ideologies that have placed asylum seekers, refugees, immigrant communities, and Muslims on the front line of the 'war on terror'. The solidarity we displayed on 15 February 2003 must be sustained and deepened in the years to come.

NOTES

1   Davis, Mike (2004) 'Planet of slums', *New Left Review*, March–April.
2   *Guardian* (2001) 'Special report: refugees in Britain', 23 May.

[149]

3   Figure quoted in Castles, Stephen, 'The new global politics and the
    emerging forced migration regime',
    <http://www.jcwi.org.uk/resources/globalisation-refugees.PDF>.
4   Ibid.
5   Ibid.
6   *Economist* (2004) 'Myths and reality', 28 February.
7   Ibid.
8   Davis, Mike (2004) 'Bush and the Great Wall', *ZNet*, 19 January,
    <http://www.zmag.org/racewatch/racewatch.cfm>.
9   Ibid.
10 Sivanandan, A (2002) 'The contours of global racism', Independent
    Race and Refugee News Network, 26 November,
    <http://www.irr.org.uk/2002/november/ak000007.html>.
11 Castles, Stephen 'The new global politics and the emerging forced
    migration regime', Joint Council for the Welfare of Immigrants,
    <http://www.jcwi.org.uk/resources/globalisation-refugees.PDF>.
12 Cummins, Will (2004) 'Muslims are a threat to our way of life', *Daily
    Telegraph*, 25 July.
13 Kundnani, Arun 'Rally around the flag', *Race and Class*, 7 April,
    <http://www.irr.org.uk/2004/april/ak000006.html>.
14 Fekete, Liz (2004) 'Anti-Muslim racism and the European security
    state', *Race and Class* special issue, July.
15 Ibid.
16 Kundnani, Arun (2004) 'Wired for war: military technology and the
    politics of fear', *Race and Class* special issue July.
17 Hörnqvist, Magnus (2004) 'The birth of public order policy', *Race and
    Class* special issue, July.

11 Privatization

and workers' rights: but neo-liberals are such *nice* people …

Bob Crow

NEO-LIBERALISM AT HOME

Neo-liberalism seems such a *nice* word. To many people the word 'liberal' conjures up a picture of reasonable, if slightly other-worldly, people in Hush Puppies bending over backwards to be nice to each other. *Chambers* dictionary defines 'liberal' as generous, noble-minded, candid, ample and free…

For working people, though, there is nothing remotely noble, generous or free about neo-liberal economic policy, for the 'freedom' of neo-liberalism is nothing more than the freedom of big capital to increase its exploitation of labour. And for capital to exercise that freedom, it must also ensure that everything possible is put in the way of working people working together to defend their public services and their jobs, pay and conditions. That is why, alongside the dismantling of economic regulation and the drive to depress wages, speed up production, lengthen hours, worsen conditions and sack 'uneconomic' workers, there is a simultaneous global attack on workers' rights.

The pattern is consistent, from Britain to Botswana, from Ukraine to Uruguay: one global capitalist's meat is millions of working people's poison. The trend was largely set in Britain, where the Conservative government of Margaret Thatcher elected in 1979 made no pretence that it represented any interests other than those of big business, and unleashed a programme of privatization in the 1980s that systematically took Britain's network of public utilities, built up over generations, and handed them, at knock-down prices, to the privateers.

Dressed up as some sort of 'people's capitalism', aerospace, gas, electricity, telecommunications and water were sold off, supposedly to thousands of ordinary people – 'Tell Sid', the expensive government ads said, conspiratorially, as if giving an exciting betting tip – but in reality to the control of transnational corporations. Of course it turned out to be a major rip-off: Sid was being mugged of something he already owned, and ended up having to pay through the nose for it. Services were deregulated and opened up to the private sector and 'market testing', and swathes of transport, catering, cleaning, direct-labour and other public-service workers found themselves working for the private sector. Local authorities, once large-scale employers of reasonably paid public-service workers, became virtual authorities, farming contracts out to the private sector.

For the grateful privateers the profits were massive, while for the workers in those industries and services, as well as those who relied on them, the results were catastrophic. Jobs were slashed, work rates increased, pay squeezed or simply cut, pension schemes robbed and undermined, and the services themselves became cash cows to be milked at the people's expense. Then came the private finance initiatives and the public–private partnerships: another way of transferring billions of public pounds into private pockets.

In order to get away with all this the Thatcher government needed to blunt the one weapon ordinary working people had that could have stopped it happening: their trade unions. So alongside the sale of the century there was wave after wave of anti-union legislation, bit by bit tightening a legal straitjacket that remains in place to this day. It is a straitjacket that leaves Britain outside international law, but that fact never bothered Thatcher, just as it does not bother Tony Blair today.

The Employment Acts of 1980, 1982, 1988, 1989 and 1990, the Trade Union Act of 1984, the 1986 Public Order Act and the 1992 Trade Union and Labour Relations (Consolidation) Act added layer after layer of legal restriction. They outlawed solidarity action, defined narrowly what was a lawful 'trade dispute', imposed lengthy balloting and notice rules for strike action, restricted picketing rights, weakened what little legal immunity there had been, outlawed the 'closed shop', gave the courts the right to seize the funds of unions deemed to be taking unlawful action, and put in place countless legal traps that could result in unions being fined or sequestrated. In short, at a time when workers needed desperately to defend themselves, the government made unions jump through hoops to take any form of industrial action at all, and made action against privatization effectively illegal.

Members of RMT (the UK's transport industry trade union) have a wealth of experience of life in privatized, deregulated and fragmented transport industries. Buses were deregulated and privatized by Thatcher in 1985. The railways were privatized by John Major's Tory government in 1996. London Underground's infrastructure was privatized by a Labour government in 2002. And now Caledonian

MacBrayne's lifeline ferry services in Scotland also face the same fragmentation and tendering.

The private sector has so far drained in excess of £10 billion in profits from the railways, and in just one year (2003–4) has claimed £100 million in 'profits' from London Underground's crumbling infrastructure, despite making no headway on promised improvements. Rail privatization has proved a disaster all round – for the public, who have seen their services decline, and for rail workers, who have been living through an industrial relations nightmare.

When RMT bus workers at Stagecoach in Devon were on strike in the summer of 2003, the company, perfectly legally, bussed in strike-breaking managers from other Stagecoach subsidiaries to drive strike-bound buses. Had the union called on trade unionists in the same subsidiaries to strike in support of their colleagues, we would have been hauled into court for 'secondary action' faster than you could say 'scab'. In today's Britain, solidarity action is fine for the bosses, but not for working people.

There are many who have sought, with the best of intentions, alternatives to the confrontation that can stem from industrial disputes. 'Social partnership' has often been put forward as one way of protecting workers' interests, in which employer and employee undertake to recognize and respect the value of each other's role. It is a path that has failed miserably for working people. Partnership agreements are often characterized by workers giving up their right to strike and holding down their own wages in exchange for some nebulous offer of job security, consultation and a confrontation-free dispute resolution procedure. Yet these 'partnerships' tend to last only as long as the boss doesn't have a better plan – like uprooting production and moving somewhere cheaper or simply tearing the agreement up.

We should all beware of bosses who call for unions to be 'reasonable' and 'modern' – for reasonable means compliant, and modern means Victorian. Time after time workers have been bitterly disappointed when the boss cites 'economic reality' as the reason to tear up the bit in the agreement about job security.

There is also now a debate under way in the British trade union movement over the European Union constitution, and there are those who believe it may offer some sort of protection to trade union rights. RMT's view is that the proposed constitution poses a threat to democracy, jobs and public services, and is no back-door way of ending or easing Britain's anti-union laws. The 800-page constitution will further instutionalize privatization and the neo-liberal economics that have helped wreck industries in Britain and turned the European Union into one of the world's low-growth regions. It would make it next to impossible to bring our transport and public services back into public ownership – and it could spell an end to a National Health Service free at the point of use. But one of the few areas over which the constitution makes clear that member states will retain sovereignty is the right to impose restrictions on the right to strike and other repressive measures – in short, the same old neo-liberal prescription.

NEO-LIBERALISM ABROAD

After her forced retirement as prime minister in 1990, Margaret Thatcher's most prominent public role was campaigning for the release of her good chum General Augusto Pinochet, who had been arrested in London in an ultimately vain attempt to put him on trial on assassination and human rights charges. At least 3,000 people 'disappeared' in Chile during the brutal 17-year reign of the fascist dictator, who led a military coup against the democratically elected socialist government of Salvador Allende in 1973.

Under Pinochet, Chile became a guinea pig for a 'monetarist' economic policy that further impoverished Chilean workers and farm labourers, and enriched foreign investors at their expense. Pinochet's approach to union rights was less subtle than Thatcher's, consisting of terror, kidnap, murder and the use of the Santiago football stadium as a concentration camp for trade unionists, socialists and democrats.

But Pinochet and Thatcher were and are political and economic soul-mates, both guided by the economic theories of the free-market guru Milton Friedman, the founder of the Chicago school of monetary economics – better known as monetarism. It was Friedman who formulated the theory that 'economic freedom' was the one freedom from which all other freedoms flowed. It is the idea that underpins the neo-liberalism that has condemned millions around the globe to poverty while the few bask in enormous wealth.

The International Monetary Fund (IMF) and the World Bank have innocent enough names – like 'liberal' they even sound vaguely benevolent and comforting, like a couple of wise great-uncles – but they have become the instruments through which the 'privatize and impoverish' economic model has been imposed worldwide. Theirs is a carrot and stick approach, one in which the carrot turns out to be another stick. These sharks offer loans to countries in debt, imposing small-print conditions that open up their economies to outside 'investors', slash public spending on health, education, housing and welfare, and turn public utilities into commodities. These 'structural adjustment programmes', as they are known, are nirvana for the transnationals, who reap super-profits by buying up water, electricity, gas, transport and telecommunications industries cheap and selling their products back expensive, while enjoying new pools of cheap and largely unregulated labour and gaining access to cheap raw materials. In Africa, Asia and Latin America, country after country has succumbed to this global protection racket, tightening the grip of the transnationals, and billions now owe their souls to the company stores.

The global drive to privatization was further spurred by the collapse of the Soviet Union and the socialist economies of Eastern Europe. What had been a political and military counterbalance to the worst excesses of imperialism was gone, leaving us with a new world order in which the 'new world' gives the orders. While the back-room theorists of neo-liberalism like Francis Fukuyama were gleefully talking about 'the end of history' – code for the final triumph of capitalism – Boris Yeltsin was selling off Siberian oil and gas and hundreds of state-owned enterprises to his friends at obscenely low prices in transactions at best scandalous, and at worst simply bent. The takeover of the publicly owned Czech motor giant Skoda by Volkswagen, the company that once embodied the Nazi dream, symbolized the supremacy in Europe of German capital – in one sense reversing the outcome of the Second World War.

And amidst the onslaught there was also a massive ideological slide – the progressive movement was well and truly on the back foot worldwide, and mainstream social-democratic parties the world over began to toe the neo-liberal line. We hear very little about Britain's 'ethical foreign policy' these days, because there isn't one. Tony Blair has talked of Africa's poverty being a stain on humanity – and so it is – yet the UK government is using public money to advise developing countries, including in Africa, how best to privatize their public services.

At the pinnacle of the pyramid of economic power sit the G8 – a cartel of hypocrites, not one of which is averse to operating behind trade barriers that would put poorer and weaker nations at risk of having their IMF loans called in, or worse. Today, policed by the neo-liberal 'consensus' of the World Trade Organization, the G8 and the key economic trading blocs, and in the new order of predatory oil wars, any government that challenges 'free' trade or resists the instructions of the IMF or World Bank now risks being labelled a dangerous tyrant and becoming another candidate for regime change.

The war against Iraq, at the cost of up to 100,000 civilian lives and massive devastation, has been followed by the systematic divvying up of the economic spoils amongst US and British-based transnationals. Support for independent trade unions in Iraq is now essential in order that the country's working people can at least win the dignity of rebuilding their own infrastructure.

Libya, until recently a bookies' favourite for next US target, has been allowed back into the 'community of nations' since it abandoned public ownership of its oil resources and its irritating tendency to use oil revenues to redistribute wealth. If there are now rumblings about regime change in Belarus, it has rather less to do with the increasingly dictatorial nature of President Alexander Lukashenko's regime and everything to do with his calling a halt to the privatization programme. After all, there are plenty of other nasty regimes around the world, from the Saud dynasty in Saudi Arabia to the government of Alvaro Uribe in Colombia, currently the most dangerous place in the world to be a trade unionist.

In exchange for US$5 billion of IMF loans over the last five years and the unconditional support of the Bush government, Uribe has privatized state-owned energy companies, telecommunications and utilities, and sacked tens of thousands of state employees. Meanwhile, he has eased the way for foreign 'investment', reduced taxes on foreign investors and increased the regressive tax burden on the poor while easing taxes for the rich. Colombian unions have been at the heart of the resistance to privatization, mass unemployment, pay cuts and other IMF-imposed austerity measures, mobilizing tens of thousands in strikes and street protests. In response, in a peculiar variation of the 'global war on terror', Uribe and his predecessors have been waging a US-financed 'war on drugs', which in reality is a war on trade unionists, carried out by right-wing paramilitaries in close cooperation with the Colombian army. In Colombia it is, in theory at least, perfectly legal to join a trade union, but last year alone some 184 trade union activists were assassinated – more than in the rest of the world combined. In the globalized economy, nothing must be allowed to get in the way of the bosses' freedom, least of all workers' rights.

There are many who look to international law, such as International Labour Organization (ILO) conventions, to rein in anti-union governments and bosses. But in the new world balance of forces, the British government can simply ignore its conventions in a way that would have been unthinkable a generation ago. Even where governments are prepared to observe the ILO and other human rights conventions they sign, the fact remains that it is governments that sign them, and not the transnational corporations that most benefit from ignoring them.

If for any self-respecting trade unionist the eleventh commandment is 'Thou shalt not cross a picket line', then for any respectable globalizing sweatshop owner it is 'Thou shalt not get found out.'

Transnationals of all sorts spend fortunes on creating their cosy, environmentally friendly, cuddly images, yet will use their economic muscle to make cynical use of countries' lax labour laws to squeeze huge profits from workers, often children, labouring for long hours in unsafe conditions for poverty wages. Household names like McDonald's and Nike, and transport giants like the First Group, recognize unions only where they have to. In one well-documented case the sportswear giant Nike tried to hide behind its outsourced contracts with third parties to turn a blind eye to the often brutal suppression of attempts by workers to organize into unions to defend themselves in Mexico. A worldwide campaign in which unions, campaigning organizations and consumers used their combined power to expose Nike ended when the sweatshop workers won the right to organize, and Nike backed down from its threat simply to end its contract with the factory.

In Britain the First Group, a major beneficiary of the privatization of bus and rail services, and a gleeful recipient of hundreds of millions of pounds in public subsidies, at least recognizes unions. But in the United States the same group's school-bus subsidiary, First Student, tells its employees that it will 'vigorously oppose any attempt by a union to organise our employees, by every legal means available'.

The shipping industry has long been a classic case of capitalist globalization, in which ship owners the world over are able to buy in the cheapest labour and exploit it mercilessly. Ship owners have flocked to the 'flags of convenience' – those national shipping registers with minimal regulation and a convenient blind eye. Largely freed from labour legislation, the owners shamelessly exploit seafarers from the poorest of nations, working them long hours in often appalling conditions for what would be below-subsistence pay. These super-exploited seafarers often report contract conditions that prohibit joining a union or contacting International Transport Workers' Federation (ITF) inspectors, on pain of being dumped, penniless, at the nearest port. Even the once-proud Red Ensign, the British merchant flag, has been dragged down the same route. Despite receiving over £100 million in British taxpayers' tonnage tax relief, British-flagged ships are increasingly following the same pattern, replacing 'expensive' British crews with low-cost overseas seafarers, even paying them below the British minimum wage while working out of British ports and in British waters.

On behalf of its maritime affiliates, the ITF campaigns tirelessly to expose the worst offenders and cajole ship owners into observing minimum standards of pay and conditions. Workers organized in one part of a transnational corporation's empire can use their own industrial muscle to help force transnationals and their subcontractors into observing minimum standards.

'WORKERS OF THE WORLD UNITE'

Strong, independent and militant trade unionism remains working people's best insurance against the bosses' drive for a low-wage, long hours economy. Wherever people fight back against privatization and free market domination, the trade union movement almost invariably plays a central role.

Against all the odds, for example, the people of the Colombian capital, Bogotá, have resisted the privatization of their water supplies, and even maintain a progressive charging system in which the wealthy pay more. Similar fights have been fought and won in Bolivia and elsewhere in Latin America, and in the political sphere there are encouraging signs as leftward shifts of varying degrees have been made since Hugo Chavez's victory in Venezuela in 1998, in Chile, Peru, Ecuador, Brazil, Argentina, and most recently in Uruguay.

There is nothing inherently wrong with a globalized economy: the idea of a worldwide division of labour for the good of humanity is a perfectly good one. But that will not be achieved through the G8's agenda of neo-liberal free market capitalism. In the struggle for the alternative – which I believe must ultimately

[161]

be a socialist one – it is time to free the unions in the same way that the neo-liberals have 'liberalized' capital. That means working for unions that are not only free of anti-union laws, but free also of self-imposed restraints, like reliance on others' respect for international law or partnership.

More than 150 years after it was first coined by Marx and Engels, the phrase 'Workers of the world unite' remains just as relevant – not just as a call for international solidarity, but as the foundation stone of any practical programme to counter the power of global capital.

USEFUL LINKS

RMT <www.rmt.org.uk>
Justice for Colombia <http://www.justiceforcolombia.org/>
Institute of Employment Rights – which has a very useful chronology of British trade union law <http://www.ier.org.uk/>
Stop the War Coalition <http://www.stopwar.org.uk>
International Centre for Trade Union Rights <http://www.ictur.labournet.org>
War on Want <http://www.waronwant.org/>
Oxfam <http://www.oxfam.org.uk/>
No Sweat <http://www.nosweat.org.uk/>

12 Poverty

Tommy Sheridan

It was the socialist R H Tawney who once wrote, 'What thinking rich people call the problem of poverty, equally thoughtful poor people call the problem of riches.' It is a statement that sits at the centre of any discussion of poverty and inequality, either at a national or international level.

Late in 2004, one of New Labour's favourite 'asylum seekers' Lakshmi Mittal jumped to the very top of the super rich league in Britain. 'Asylum seekers' like Mittal and Roman Abramovich are not fleeing violence, torture or persecution. They flee from more rigorous tax regimes to domicile themselves in Britain where their top-notch accountants can better arrange their various accounts into tax havens and thus avoid even Britain's puny tax levels for the billionaires.

Thus the real scroungers in society are not the asylum seekers disallowed from working and fleeing persecution, but the fat cat minority fleeing tougher tax regimes and who seek to keep as much of their money as possible. It's a kind of protection racket for the twenty-first century. The super rich like Lakshmi Mittal with £12 billion make big donations to the New Tory Labour party and in return top-rate taxes are frozen, tax haven loopholes are ignored and rewards for rich pension schemes are assured.

If you add the wealth of Britain's richest ten together, it now amounts to £54.02 billion.[1] How bloody obscene. The 129 Members of the Scottish Parliament (of which I am one) debate and discuss how best to spend our annual budget of around £25 billion. We have the worst poverty rates in Britain and among the worst in Europe. One in three children are born into poverty-income-level households, while 25 per cent of senior citizens live below the officially defined poverty line.

Our annual budget of £25 billion has to cater for over five million men, women and children. The ten richest between them live on more than double that. Ten individuals have more money than the whole health service in Britain. Ten people share out a pot of gold bigger than the annual budgets of whole countries.

Of course such obscene inequality of wealth is magnified on a world scale. A few hundred billionaires own more wealth than half the world. Three billion people live on less income together than the world's richest 300. If such facts don't make you angry, I despair at your lack of compassion and basic human decency. A fraction of the wealth concentrated in the hands of the few hundred billionaires could transform the lives of those suffering and dying from poverty-related diseases like cholera, malaria and diarrhoea, which claim thousands of children prematurely every single day.

Of course a proper distribution of resources and taxes across the world would eradicate poverty and its various killer diseases. That so much of our world and its population are poor while so few are obscenely rich is not some state of affairs designated by nature. It is a problem made by humans, and the only barrier to tackling the problem is the lack of political will at both a national and international level.

The political class in most countries is out of touch with such problems and oblivious to the severity of the problem. Their pay and working conditions provide an adequate cover from the chill cold poverty in their countries at large. In Scotland the average income of all taxpayers according to Inland

Revenue is £19,474.29 per annum.[2] Yet 635,000 taxpayers, as well as those reliant solely on state benefits and state pensions, live on less than £10,000 a year. That's 25.92 per cent of the taxpaying population and 12.56 per cent of the total population. A massive 1,641,000 earn less than £20,000 a year, representing 67 per cent of the taxpaying population and 32.5 per cent of the total population.

Backbench MSPs are paid £50,300 a year. Only 88,000 individuals earn more than £50,000. That means politicians in Scotland earn more than 96 per cent of other earners and live on an income bracket that places them in the top 2 per cent of the population. How grotesquely unrepresentative!

In the middle of 2003 the scale and continued expansion in the earnings and wealth gap was exposed. Research revealed in the *Guardian* (31 July 2003) showed average pay for the bosses of big companies rose seven times faster than average earnings for ordinary workers. The average wage increase for the bosses was 23 per cent but for the workers only 3 per cent, and this at a time when stocks and share prices had tumbled by 24 per cent.

Thus the average pay of a top boss in Britain rose to £1,677,685, including bonuses and other perks. Their actual basic average was £596,817. The 23 per cent wage rise last year followed a 28 per cent rise the year before.

While many Tesco workers rely on means-tested benefits like Council Tax Benefit and Housing Benefit to survive, all eight full-time directors of Tesco were paid more than £1 million. Their total wage bill together topped £20 million.

The gaping chasm between workers' pay and that of their bosses is extended even further in retirement. Currently workers are being lectured to work harder and longer while saving more. Meanwhile the fat cats of the world, like Bob Mendelsohn, can walk away from Royal and Sun Alliance after sacking 12,000 staff and presiding over a 90 per cent fall in share price for the company, to 'make ends meet' on a £1.4 million pay-off, excluding an annual pension of £354,000.

Such huge salaries for the bosses allow the likes of Sir Richard Sykes, former chairman of GlaxoSmithKline, to put £15.2 million aside for his pension, a pot that generates £729,000 in income to help him 'prepare' for retirement. A total of eight directors in this corporation have pension pots of more than £10 million each. No need for them to work longer! Meanwhile the average pension for 'ordinary' workers would hardly pay the monthly sherry or port bills for the super-rich minority.

As a socialist I believe each country's natural wealth and resources should be available to deploy for the benefit of all its citizens, not for the super-exploitation of the tiny privileged few. If the major sectors of each country's economies were publicly owned and democratically administered, the material wealth of all could be radically improved in a socially just and environmentally sustainable manner. Unfortunately not everyone yet shares this approach to economics and politics.

The more people become aware of the obscene inequality of income that haunts our country and the world, hopefully the numbers willing to support such fundamental political change will grow. Instead of the creed of greed, satisfaction of human need and the promotion of human cooperation, solidarity and love would become the order of the day.

NOTES

1 LRD Fact Service, 66:43, 28 October 2004.
2 Scottish Parliament Information and Resource Centre (SPICe) letter to Tommy Sheridan MSP, 30 September 2004.

13 Debt:
the debt crisis and the campaign to end it

Vicki Clayton

The debt crisis has caused a massive transfer of wealth from the poor to the rich, from the developing South to the developed North.

Between 1983–93 it is estimated that US$300 billion was transferred from the South to the North. At the same time indebted poor countries have been unable to meet the needs of their populations. The UN estimates that seven million children die unnecessarily each year. They die of diseases that can be cured and from unclean water that could be made safe. The debt crisis can be held responsible for the needless deaths of millions of citizens across the world, and debt is still taking lives. Were debt repayments spent instead on tackling poverty, many of these lives could be saved.

The debt campaign in the United Kingdom has traditionally – and in many ways successfully – chosen to try to influence rather than oppose successive G8 summits. In 1998 the G8 Summit was held in Birmingham. About 70,000 people formed a human chain in peaceful protest around the summit, calling for the cancellation of the unpayable debts of the world's poorest countries. Since then, through dogged determination,

[167]

campaigners have applied persistent pressure to the United Kingdom and other G8 governments to force debt onto the political agenda and, vitally, to keep it there.

In the United Kingdom the debt campaign has enjoyed a series of small victories through targeted lobbying. Debt campaigners are aware that, although we may try to influence decision makers, the current government actively courts 'civil society'. There is real and present danger of co-option. We have been resolute in not letting grand promises blinker our vision for a world without debt. And we remain acutely aware of the harmful conditions attached to loans and debt relief, which promote laissez-faire capitalism, which many poor countries are forced to adhere to.

As the G8 Summit once more returns to the UK in 2005 – seven years after the momentous display of solidarity between civil society in the North and indebted populations in the South – campaign and lobby groups across the world raise their hopes that this time a real and lasting commitment to cancel unpayable debt will be made and delivered upon.

THE ORIGINS OF THE DEBT CRISIS

The debt crisis grew from the legacy of decades of reckless and sometimes corrupt lending and borrowing from which the poor did not benefit, made worse by a global economic system rigged to reward the rich.

The origins of the debt crisis lie in the oil crisis of the 1970s. In 1973, oil-producing countries hiked their prices by 400 per cent. This action, taken through the Organization of the Petroleum Exporting Countries (OPEC), was in response to a threat to their profits from the devaluation of the dollar, and in reaction to Western support for Israel. Wealthy oil-producing countries deposited their capital in Western banks which, suddenly finding themselves awash with money, lent generously and sometimes recklessly, at a very low rate of interest, to developing countries. During the 1980s as the world economy continued to slow, interest rates rocketed, requiring borrower countries to slash public spending in order to keep up repayments. They were forced to cut back on health, education and other vital social services to finance debt repayment. This continues today.

Much of the existing debt has arisen as a result of the high spending of authoritarian and militaristic regimes. During the Cold War, Western creditors lent indiscriminately to such regimes to keep them on-side. Where democracies have replaced such dictatorships they have also inherited their debts – debts which in turn threaten to undermine democracy.

A huge amount of lending has supported large-scale building projects such as dams and power stations. These are known as 'prestige' projects, as they look impressive and initially add to the status of borrowing regimes and lenders. The problem is that they are often badly conceived, do nothing for the poor (and sometimes harm them through, for example, forced relocations), and are a magnet for corruption.

In 1982 Mexico threatened to default on – refuse to pay – its debts. This sent shock waves through the international financial system, and creditors took action to protect themselves from losses. The international finance institutions – the International Monetary Fund (IMF) and World Bank, controlled by the world's richest countries – stepped in as international debt collection agencies. Poor countries became trapped in a vicious cycle of negotiating new loans to pay back old debts. This quick-fix approach has deepened and prolonged their debt problems.

Today about a third of poor-country debt is owed to the IMF and World Bank.[1] Both these institutions are answerable to their shareholders – national governments – and voting rights are allocated according to financial contribution. The group of seven richest countries (the G8 minus Russia) controls over half the votes, and each country has an executive director appointed to the board. The United States holds 17 per cent of the voting share, and has the power of veto over the World Bank. By contrast Mozambique controls 0.1 per cent of the vote. Two executive directors represent the interests of 46 African countries.

The IMF and World Bank have power to reschedule and reduce debts, and have used this power to impose reforms on developing countries that have done little to help their struggling economies and have often hurt the poor.

The United Nations Conference on Trade and Development (UNCTAD) looked at the experience of the world's poorest countries and concluded that IMF/World Bank policies were at least partially responsible for widespread suffering and increased poverty, as well as a fall in per capita income in sub-Saharan Africa as a whole.[2]

CONDITIONALITY

Creditors set conditions for new loans and for debt relief which often harm poor country citizens. For decades heavily indebted countries have had to comply with 'structural adjustment' programmes that lead to cuts in public welfare, unaffordable fees for basic services, mass unemployment, exorbitant price increases and lower export earnings. Yet rich countries have benefited from structural adjustment: our companies have bought poor-country public assets at bargain prices, and we enjoy basic commodities, such as coffee, on the cheap.

Many of the criticisms levelled at IMF and World Bank loans

from the developing South and from Northern campaigners stress the unfair and often harmful conditions attached to both loans and debt relief programmes. Each IMF loan has 160 conditions attached, while to qualify for debt relief, countries have to adhere to the conditions of the World Bank's 'Poverty Reduction and Growth Facility'. These conditions are very similar to those enforced by structural adjustment programmes and include the following.

- **Cutting social spending:** countries are forced to reduce expenditures on health, education and the like.
- **Shrinking government:** countries must reduce budget expenses by trimming payroll and programmes.
- **Increasing interest rates:** to combat inflation, they must increase the interest charged for credit and awarded to savings.
- **Eliminating regulations on foreign ownership of resources and businesses.**
- **Eliminating tariffs:** countries stop collecting taxes on imports. These taxes are often applied to goods which would compete with domestically produced goods.
- **Cutting subsidies for basic goods:** countries must reduce government expenditures supporting a reduced price for bread, petroleum and so on.
- **Reorienting economies from subsistence to exports:** governments must give incentives for farmers to produce cash crops (coffee, cotton and so on) for foreign markets rather than food for domestic ones; encourage manufacturing to focus on simple assembly (often clothing) for export rather than manufacturing for their own country; and encourage the extraction of valuable mineral resources.

DEBT AND TRADE: TWO SIDES OF THE SAME COIN

Debt is also inextricably linked with trade imbalances. It is both a cause and a consequence of poor trade performance in many developing countries.

To repay debts most poor countries are dependent on income from the export of crops and raw materials. The world trading system keeps the prices of these commodities low and unstable, while rich countries enjoy huge profits by manufacturing or processing them. In the 1980s creditors pressured indebted poor countries to over-produce crops and raw materials, leading to a collapse in prices. This meant the harder poor countries worked, the less they were able to earn to repay debts. Problems arising from collapsing commodity prices continue. During 2000–1 the world price of coffee fell by 60 per cent, creating serious balance of payments difficulties for Ethiopia, Honduras, Nicaragua, Rwanda, Uganda and Tanzania.[3]

Rich countries continue to discriminate against poor countries that try to add value to raw materials by processing or manufacturing them. The cost of Northern trade barriers to developing countries is estimated at US$700 billion a year in lost export earnings.[4] Rich countries subsidize their producers, particularly in agriculture, making it impossible for poor countries to compete. Lost income as a result of rich country protectionism undermines poor countries' ability to repay debts. Yet as creditors, rich countries insist that indebted poor countries expose themselves to unrestrained market forces. James Wolfensohn, President of the World Bank, 2002[5] makes the following point:

> World-wide, agricultural subsidies in developed countries to the tune of $350 billion a year are seven times what countries spend on development assistance and

roughly equivalent to the entire GDP of sub-Saharan Africa. Those subsidies are crippling Africa's chances to export its way out of poverty. Rich countries must dramatically reduce these subsidies.

THE IMPACT OF DEBT: THE HUMAN COST

Unsustainable levels of unpayable debt reinforce a model of globalization that is based on neo-liberal economics. It is this neo-liberal economic system that is working against the people, as indebted poor-country economies are controlled by multilateral institutions and do not reflect their citizens' needs. This divorce between economies and societies is at the core of the problem with our current global democracy, and the debt crisis has provided an excuse to enforce this. Now global markets dominate national democracies and tell them what to do. Governments are taking instruction from global markets rather than their people. The effects are devastating.

The conditions attached to loans and debt relief mechanisms have been harmful to youthful, emerging economies, and it is the citizens of these countries who continue to pay the price.

Health

The government of Zambia, Southern Africa, spends almost 25 per cent of its budget on debt repayments. This is three times the amount spent on health care. Nearly 20 per cent of adults are living with HIV/AIDS in Zambia, and 86 per cent of the population live below the poverty line. Life expectancy in Zambia is 33 – the lowest life expectancy of any country in the world.[6] It is estimated that 45 per cent of people in the Copperbelt province, one of the wealthiest regions of the country, can no longer afford to take their children to the doctor as a result of user fees and job losses from the privatization of Zambia Consolidated Copper Mines.[7]

There are 18 doctors for 100,000 people in Guyana, South America, and 18 per cent of the population is under-nourished. Yet Guyana pays four times more on debt than health.[8]

Education

In Burkina Faso, where 66 per cent of men and 90 per cent of women are illiterate, twice as much is spent on debt service as on education, and only one-third of children attend school.[9]

Water

In Manila, Philippines, the urban water supply was handed over to a subsidiary of Thames Water. This led to a sevenfold increase in user fees in the east and five-fold increase in the west. The company has since gone bankrupt, leaving 4,000 overdue repairs and a cholera epidemic.

In Ghana, West Africa, 70 per cent of people live on less than US$1 a day and 30 per cent lack access to safe drinking water. Under pressure from creditors the government has embarked on a hasty privatization programme of the public urban water system, which has resulted in a near-doubling of water fees.[10]

THE CAMPAIGNS

The Jubilee campaign

The Jubilee 2000 campaign was launched in late 1997. It was a coming together in a coalition of several strands already campaigning on the debt issue – in the UK chiefly the Debt Crisis Network and the major aid agencies. The idea caught on, and very quickly the campaign became worldwide, with Jubilee campaigns in many countries of the world both North and South. Its petition was the biggest ever, and gained a place in the Guinness Book of Records. It gathered over 24 million signatures in 160 countries.

In the United Kingdom a great breakthrough was made in 1998, with the human chain around the G8 summit meeting in Birmingham that was mentioned earlier. Tony Blair came out and met with the leaders, and for the first time the international debt issue got on to the G7 agenda, where it has been ever since.

The following year at the G8 Summit in Cologne, the G8 leaders promised a figure of US$100 billion in debt cancellation, a third of the figure Jubilee 2000 was campaigning for, but at least a step in the right direction. Since then, successive summits have offered very little of substance, and the promise of US$100 billion of debt relief has not been delivered.

The Jubilee 2000 coalition was always conceived of as a short-term campaign – its aim was to achieve debt cancellation by the millennium. It was virtually built into its constitution that it would stop at the end of 2000. Yet despite the promises made again and again in Cologne in 1999, voices from Jubilee South told Northern campaign partners that while they appreciated what had been done, we were naïve to think that so big an issue could be resolved in so short a time. They were insistent that the campaign must go on, and that we in the North must not let it stop.

In the United Kingdom in 2001, Drop the Debt was established as a one-year last-push campaign for the G8 Summit in Genoa. Genoa at first promised so much, until an Italian general election returned a right-wing government, and anti-globalization demonstrators and the Italian police brought violence on to the streets. Also in 2001, the Jubilee Debt Campaign and Jubilee Scotland emerged in the United Kingdom to take over where Drop the Debt left off. Most countries that had a Jubilee 2000 campaign have successor organizations which together continue to campaign for debt cancellation for the world's poorest countries.

HIPC: A FLAWED PROCESS

The Heavily Indebted Poor Country (HIPC) programme was proposed by the World Bank and IMF, and agreed by governments around the world in 1996. It promised a lasting exit from debt troubles for poor countries, yet nine years since its conception it is clear that poor countries are still being strangled by their debts. The reason for HIPC's failure is basic flaws in the way the debt relief programme is designed.

Debt relief calculated using the wrong yardstick

Under HIPC, if a country's debts are more than one and a half times its exports, they are considered 'unsustainable' and action is taken to take its debt level below this threshold. The problem lies in using exports as the yardstick. This tells us very little about how much of the government budget in a poor country is being used for debt service. The Jubilee campaign argues that it is far better to look at how much money a poor country needs to tackle poverty effectively, and to cut debts accordingly.

Debt relief decisions based on flawed IMF/World Bank predictions

IMF and World Bank predictions for economic growth in developing countries are often wildly optimistic and seem to have little regard for past experience. Yet it is on these predictions that decisions about how much debt to cancel are based. Predictions also discount the possibility of export price collapses and natural disasters, such as hurricanes and flooding.

Poverty reduction – who is in control?

Countries taking part in HIPC are asked to produce a Poverty Reduction Strategy Paper (PRSP) in consultation with citizens' groups, which describes how they will use the money saved by debt relief to tackle poverty. Although this is sound in theory, in practice these papers must be approved by creditors, and consequently poor-country governments draw them up in accordance with IMF and World Bank preferences. Citizens' groups in developing countries also complain that the requirement to consult them is often overlooked or paid lip service. The content of PRSPs is often similar to the discredited 'structural adjustment' programmes they replace.

Sins of omission

The HIPC programme is aimed at the most heavily indebted and poorest countries in the world. Some desperately poor countries have not qualified for debt relief because of conflict or extreme instability. There are others, however, that have been mysteriously excluded in spite of high levels of debt and poverty. Nigeria, where 20 per cent of the population of sub-Saharan Africa lives, is the most glaring exclusion, having been on the original HIPC list and then scored off. Bangladesh and Jamaica are others.

Light at the end of the tunnel

Although problems remain with the current debt relief mechanism, and commitments to cancel debt are slow in being realized, where debt has been cancelled it has made a real difference. A recent study of 10 countries that had received some debt relief showed:

- In 1998 education spending was US$929 million. Today it is US$1,306 million, more than twice what is being spent on debt service.
- Mozambique has introduced a free immunization programme for children.
- School fees for primary education have been abolished in Uganda, Malawi, Zambia, Tanzania and rural areas of Benin.

WHO HAS THE POWER TO CANCEL THE DEBT AND CHANGE THE RULES?

Without 100 per cent debt cancellation, fair trade and an increase in aid, the world's poorest countries will fail to reach the Millennium Development Goal targets by 2015.[11] The World Bank, IMF and the G8 have the power and the resources to cancel the debt and change the rules. Ultimately the stumbling block is political will.

If we are to succeed in finding real and lasting solutions to global poverty, debt cancellation must be delivered. It is the G8 countries that can provide the political will to make this happen. The G8 countries hold half the votes on the boards of the IMF and World Bank. This means that ultimately, the G8 have the power to cancel the debts of the poorest countries not only to their own governments, but also to the World Bank and IMF.[12]

If the World Bank and IMF were to cancel all debts owed to them by the poorest countries (37 per cent of all their debt) this would make a tremendous difference. There is strong evidence to suggest that both these institutions are over-capitalized, and can fund the cancellation of debts owed to them without external assistance and without harming their lending operations and credit ratings.[13] There is growing support among civil society groups for a proposal to sell off some of the IMF's gold reserves in order to fund this debt cancellation. Selling off just 5 million ounces of IMF gold per year is an affordable and realistic way to finance debt relief for poor countries.[14]

The moral argument for debt cancellation is clear. The creditors' repayment methods are unethical: repayment interest rates are above the market norm, and debt levels can consequently be five times the value of the original loan. To pay this debt in full means grave economic dislocation and increased poverty, as harmful conditions attached to loans and debt relief programmes have led to increased unemployment and reduced spending on health and education. Coupled with this, ever-worse terms of trade for the South mean greater economic advantage for the North.[15]

The moral and economic argument can be won. What we need to continue to fight for is the political will to make this happen. Campaigners will continue to argue for 100 per cent debt cancellation for the world's poorest countries, and argue that:

1. The unpayable debts of the world's poorest countries should be cancelled in full, by fair and transparent means.
2. Any resources necessary to achieve such cancellation should be in addition to, and not drawn from, the funds required to meet existing targets for overseas aid.
3. The international financial institutions must stop requiring poor countries to implement harmful economic policies, such as privatization and liberalization, as a condition for granting debt relief.

4. Full multilateral debt cancellation should be rapidly delivered, particularly given that many countries have already demonstrated that money freed up by debt relief has been spent on poverty reduction.

5. Future development funding for the world's poorest countries should have a strong bias towards grants (without harmful conditions), until such a time as they can reasonably be expected to bear low-interest loans.

The campaign to cancel unpayable debt will continue across the world. Jubilee 2000 succeeded in mobilizing public opinion, and civil society will continue to campaign for change until the injustice of the debt crisis is resolved. At each annual meeting of the G8 governments, debt campaigners will continue to press for change. Now is the time to make our governments accountable, and ensure they feel the public pressure which will in turn provide the political will to cancel unpayable debt.

We can make a change, but it's a global thing. We are not alone.

Lebaogang Seakgoe, aged 15, South Africa

NOTES

1   Drop the Debt (2001) 'Reality check', Drop the Debt, April, p 26.
2   World Development Movement (2002), *Campaign Briefing: A challenge to the G7 Finance Ministers meeting in Canada. Fiddling, while Africa suffers*, WDM, June, p 7.
3   Oxfam (2002) *Debt Relief and the HIV/AIDS Crisis in Africa*, Oxfam, 3 June, p 19.
4   Trade Justice Movement, *Founding Statement*, TJM <http:www.tjm.org.uk/about/statement.shtml>.
5   World Bank press release, 26 June 2002.
6   Jubilee Plus (2001) 'HIPC – flogging a dead process', September.

7 Christian Aid (1998) *Field of Graves*, London, September, p 14.

8 Jubilee Plus (2001) 'HIPC – flogging a dead process', September
   <http:/www.jubileeplus.org/analysis/reports/
   flogging_process_text.htm>.

9 Greenhill, R (2002) Jubilee Research at the New Economics Foundation
   and Jubilee Debt Campaign, 'The unbreakable link: debt relief and the
   millennium development goals', Jubilee Research at the New Economics
   Foundation and Jubilee Debt Campaign, February, p 14.

10 Amenga-Etego, R N (undated) *CAP of Water Campaign. Water Privati-
    sation in Ghana: The Reality and the mirage*, CAP of Water Campaign,
    p. 2.

11 An internationally agreed set of targets that aim by 2015 to halve the
    number of people living on less than a dollar a day.

12 Drop the Debt (2001) *Frequently Asked Questions*, factsheet, Drop the
    Debt.

13 Jubilee Research for Debt and Development Coalition Ireland (2003)
    Can the World Bank and IMF Cancel 100% of Poor Country Debt?, p 4.

14 Sony Kapoor Jubilee Research for Debt and Development Coalition
    Ireland (2004) *IMF Gold Sales and Multilateral Debt Cancellation*,
    September, p 2.

15 Potter, George Ann (2000) *Deeper than Debt*, Latin American Bureau,
    London, p 78.

14 Health
and HIV/AIDS: fine words and fatal indifference

Ronald Labonte, Ted Schrecker and David McCoy

HIV infection has devastated sub-Saharan Africa (SSA), lowering life expectancies by ten years or more in some countries, wiping out recent gains in population health, and causing social dislocation that is hard to comprehend. For example Malawi, one of the world's poorest countries with a population of just 10.5 million, must address the needs of an estimated 500,000 children who have already lost at least one parent to AIDS.[1]

HIV is not the only infectious disease challenge for SSA. Malaria kills close to a million people a year, mostly children less than five years old; tuberculosis kills twice as many people worldwide, and is 'the leading cause of death in HIV-infected individuals in Africa'.[2] In addition, the region faces a 'double burden of disease' created by rapid increases in non-communicable diseases such as cardiovascular disease and diabetes. In this chapter we concentrate on infectious diseases, because control is necessary, although not sufficient, for avoiding 'medical poverty traps',[3] in which illness drives households and communities into poverty and threatens to do the same to entire countries.

The G8[4] have made bold promises about improving global health, committing (in 2000) to an ambitious agenda of reducing the damage done by HIV, tuberculosis and malaria.[5] Using methods explained elsewhere,[6] we examine these promises in light of three questions. Have they been met? Are they adequate to the need? And are they compatible with the market-driven development policies and world view that the G8 continue to promote?

HEALTH SYSTEMS AND INFECTION CONTROL

Most health care systems in SSA are fragile in the extreme, and indicators like declining child immunization rates show that many are deteriorating. The most immediate problem is lack of money: excluding South Africa, countries in the region spend less than US$14 per capita on health each year.[7] Although the G8 noted in 2001 that '[s]trong national health systems will continue to play a key role in the delivery of effective prevention, treatment and care',[8] they have not adequately addressed financing issues.

The World Health Organization's (WHO's) Commission on Macroeconomics and Health (CMH) estimated that a minimal package of essential health interventions for the world's poor countries, including all of SSA, would save 'at least 8 million lives each year by the end of this decade'.[9] This package of interventions, including only partial coverage for key HIV, malaria and tuberculosis treatments, would require US$22.1 billion from the industrialized world in 2007, rising to US$30.7 billion in 2015[10] – compared with estimated health-related development assistance from all countries (not just the G8) of US$8.1 billion in 2002.[11]

As a rule, commitments to improving global health fall short of the level of need by an order of magnitude. Created in 2001, the Global Fund for AIDS, Tuberculosis and Malaria was promoted as 'a quantum leap in the fight against infectious diseases and to break the vicious cycle between disease and poverty'.[12] By September 2004, the G8 had pledged and contributed US$4.24 billion to the fund, not including contributions made through the European Commission.[13] This sounds like a lot of money, but the CMH concluded that, to be effective, the Global Fund will require US$8 billion *per year* by 2007, and US$12 billion per year by 2015. In June 2004 the Global Fund's Director of External Relations warned that 'unless our major donors make renewed and increased commitments, it is hard to see how any new round [of funding] could be financed in 2005 or 2006'.[14] WHO's '3 by 5' campaign to initiate anti-retroviral (ARV) treatment for three million people by the end of 2005 is similarly threatened by underfunding.[15] Moreover, University of British Columbia researchers estimate that just under *nine million* people outside the industrialized world *already* need access to ARVs,[16] three times the WHO's ambitious target.

Lack of human resources is a further constraint. Indispensable doctors and nurses are themselves falling victim to HIV or leaving for the industrialized world, a 'brain drain' that is becoming the most formidable obstacle to rebuilding and strengthening health systems.[17] According to the *New York Times*, 'In Malawi, afflicted with one of Africa's most severe nursing shortages, almost two-thirds of the nursing jobs in the public health system are vacant.'[18] Brain drain is driven by such factors as inadequate salary, poor facilities, few basic medicines and other therapies, and safety concerns. Also, active recruitment by countries like

Canada, the United Kingdom and the United States means they save money by hiring health professionals trained in much poorer countries.[19] These processes are replicated within SSA and other developing regions when 'vertical' disease programmes financed by external donors attract health professionals with higher salaries and better career options,[20] unintentionally undermining the basic health infrastructure.

In the short run, the G8 can do little about the direct effect of HIV on health systems except increase support for HIV prevention, treatment and research. They can and should provide drastically increased levels of stable multi-year health system funding through donor agencies, and devise shared reporting systems to cut down administrative work that diverts people and resources from clinical activities. They should also pursue the recommendation in the health strategy under the New Partnership for Africa's Development (NEPAD), the 'made-in-Africa' statement endorsed by the G8 in 2002, for an international agreement to deal with the impacts of health professionals' migration from poor to rich countries.[21]

Since Hippocrates, a basic medical axiom has been 'first, do no harm', yet 'reforms' promoted by the G8, directly and through the World Bank and the International Monetary Fund (IMF), have actually undermined national health systems. Demands that health systems become financially 'sustainable' have increased reliance on user fees and cost recovery, although the revenues raised are meagre and the barriers to access often substantial.[22] In 1999, a Ghanaian columnist succinctly described the choices facing the poor in that country's health care system as 'pay cash or carry death'.[23] The process of turning health care (and nearly everything else) over to the market must in turn be understood as part of a broader development policy orientation that has deepened economic differences both among and within countries.[24]

MARKETS VERSUS BASIC HEALTH NEEDS

Access to essential medicines illustrates the tension between markets and basic needs. Without strong international protection of intellectual property (IP) rights like patents, 'knowledge-based' industries such as pharmaceuticals cannot maximize their global profits. Strong patent protection may or may not be essential to financing innovative medical research,[25] but it does enable manufacturers to keep the cost of life-saving drugs unaffordably high. The US government, and US-based multinational corporations, were the prime movers behind the Agreement on Trade-Related Aspects of Intellectual Property (TRIPS), which seeks to harmonize IP protection throughout the World Trade Organization (WTO). George Washington University political scientist Susan Sell comments that corporate influence on US policy during the negotiating process was so extensive that 'in effect, twelve corporations made public law for the world'.[26] They included pharmaceutical giants Bristol-Myers (now Bristol-Myers Squibb), Merck and Pfizer.

As a middle-income country, Brazil has provided free access to ARVs because of provisions in its patent laws that permit 'compulsory licensing' of pharmaceuticals, a strategy credited with reducing AIDS deaths and hospital admissions for opportunistic infections.[27] In December 1997, new South African legislation provided for compulsory licensing. The US government challenged the Brazilian provisions through the WTO in 2000, and also aggressively but unsuccessfully pressured South Africa to withdraw its legislation. By 2001, the US and South African subsidiaries of major pharmaceutical firms had retreated from the most visible aspects of their opposition. Meanwhile a high-profile international campaign for access to essential medicines had two more important outcomes.

First, the major drug firms negotiated lower prices for patented drugs sold in developing countries. Second, the November 2001 Doha ministerial meeting of WTO member countries produced a declaration that clearly supported limiting patent protection under TRIPS when necessary to protect public health.[28] Reportedly because of US intransigence, only in August 2003 did the WTO General Council clearly indicate that both compulsory licensing and imports of generic medicines produced under such licences by countries lacking their own production capacity ('parallel imports', in WTO-speak) are permissible.[29]

These developments represent a clear victory for a coalition of developing-country governments and civil society organizations, yet concerns persist about implementation. Canada, the first G8 country to amend its own legislation to allow domestic firms to produce generic versions of patented drugs for export, was lauded for its leadership but criticized for the small number of drugs initially covered under the legislative amendments.[30] More importantly, slow and burdensome procedures that developing countries must follow in order to make use of the Doha provisions, along with informal pressures placed on governments not to use them, may neutralize their positive impact on the ground.[31]

What about priorities for medical research? ARVs are on the market in the first place because rich people get AIDS; sufferers in the industrialized world provided an attractive market and a political constituency for publicly funded research on the disease. Pharmaceutical firms, however, now provide 41.5 per cent of *all* health research spending worldwide,[32] which means many infectious diseases receive little attention. Regardless of patent protection, sufferers often are too poor to constitute an attractive market.

For instance, no new drugs have been approved for treating trypanosomiasis (sleeping sickness) since 1981, although more than 300,000 people are infected in SSA every year, and evidence exists of increasing drug resistance.[33] Researchers associated with Médecins sans Frontières (MSF) found that of 1,393 new drugs marketed between 1975 and 1999, only 16 were for tropical diseases and tuberculosis.[34] This reflects the so-called '10/90 gap': roughly 10 per cent of health research spending addresses 90 per cent of the global burden of disease, overwhelmingly outside the industrialized world. The MSF researchers argued for a 'paradigm shift in health and research and development policy'. However, the G8 have been conspicuously silent on such questions as who will hold IP rights to the results of the Global HIV Vaccine Enterprise announced at the 2004 Summit. A report in *The Lancet* suggests that the Enterprise will aim to raise US$1–5 billion per year, as against current HIV vaccine research funding of US$550 million per year,[35] but it is unclear whether the funds will truly represent new money, or will be diverted from other health-related areas of aid budgets.

INFLATION, DEBT AND ECONOMIC RESTRUCTURING

Medical anthropologist Brooke Grundfest Schoepf, a specialist in the spread of HIV/AIDS in Zaire (now the Democratic Republic of Congo) and Malawi, observes that by 1988 people in Zaire 'had another name for AIDS (SIDA in French) that encapsulated their understanding of its social epidemiology', which included rapid social change, endemic economic insecurity and the subordination of women: '*Salaire Insuffisant Depuis des Années*'.[36] The alternative acronym eloquently captures the relations among HIV infection, desperation and economic insecurity, and suggests that we need to look outside

[188]

the health care box in order to understand the epidemic and associated policy failures.

Peter Piot, the Executive Director of the United Nations AIDS Programme, warned at the 2004 International AIDS Conference that 'Africa's crippling debt must be relieved – the $15 billion annually that disappears down the money pit. That is four times more than is spent on health and education – the building blocks of the AIDS response.'[37] To oversimplify greatly, in the 1970s and early 1980s the governments of many newly independent African countries borrowed money, from private lenders and (especially) from multilateral agencies like the World Bank and the IMF, to address the revenue squeeze resulting from declining commodity prices and rising energy costs. Domestic economic mismanagement, cronyism and capital flight contributed to the need to borrow, but these are hardly unique to the African context. By the late 1980s, many of these countries were reorganizing their policies along lines specified by the World Bank and IMF, in return for 'structural adjustment' loans designed primarily to ensure that national governments could repay at least some of their debt. In 1987, a UNICEF-sponsored study showed that policies adopted by ten countries, including Botswana, Ghana and Zimbabwe, were undermining child health.[38] The study's call for 'adjustment with a human face' was generally ignored, then and later, despite subsequent research confirming the negative effects of structural adjustment on determinants of health in SSA.[39]

Belatedly, the industrialized world has implemented the enhanced Heavily Indebted Poor Countries (HIPC) initiative, which offers partial debt cancellation (through the World Bank and IMF) to 32 African countries. However, even complete debt cancellation for these countries would not make available enough resources to meet basic needs related to health.[40] In addition, eligibility for enhanced HIPC requires preparing a

Poverty Reduction Strategy Paper (PRSP) for approval by the World Bank and IMF, and the macroeconomic policy commitments made in those papers look a lot like the demands of structural adjustment.[41] A recent study by University of Sussex researchers pointed out that some PRSPs 'include trade-related conditions that are more stringent, in terms of requiring more, or faster, or deeper liberalization, than WTO provisions to which the respective country has agreed'.[42] So some of the poorest countries in the world are being asked to open up their markets even faster, with the associated economic insecurity, erosion of fiscal capacity (as tax revenues decline) and social dislocation, despite the industrialized world's reluctance to accept their exports.

The G8 continue to promote global market integration, declaring (in 2001) that 'drawing the poorest countries into the global economy is the surest way to address their fundamental aspirations'.[43] They neglect the crucial issue of on whose terms those countries are to be integrated into international networks of trade and investment. As economic historian Ha-Joon Chang notes, current prescriptions for growth and development amount to 'kicking away the ladder': they preclude policies favouring domestic producers that the industrialized world followed on its own path to wealth, and similar policies that explain the rapid growth of the so-called Asian tigers.[44]

HEALTH AND THE POLITICAL ECONOMY OF EXPENDABLE POPULATIONS

Meeting health needs in SSA (and indeed, in many poorer parts of the world) will require massive transfers of wealth from rich countries to poor, but expecting the G8 to adopt a needs-based approach to health in the developing world (notwithstanding recent pledges for debt cancellation and increased aid by the United Kingdom and a few other G8 countries) requires purposeful naïveté. The G8 came together (as the G6) in 1975 to coordinate national policy responses to a crisis of profitability resulting from sluggish growth in the industrialized economies, compounded by the 1973–4 oil price increases.[45] Their approach became a relentless attack on workers' post-war economic gains, combining tight monetary policy with labour market 'flexibility': what a *Wall Street Journal* writer called 'the just-in-time workforce'.[46] The attack has continued: at the 1999 Summit, after two decades' experience with downsizing and growing economic polarization in their own economies, the G7 'strongly support[ed] the elimination of structural rigidities' in labour markets,[47] saying 'it is vital to strike a sustainable balance between social support programs and greater personal responsibility and initiative'.[48]

Within this market-oriented frame of reference, health as a human need is irrelevant. Health matters only as cost of production (workers want health benefits, and a few still have the bargaining power to make this demand effectively), a profit centre (in the case of privatized health care or health insurance), a source of political demands for publicly financed services, or as an investment (healthy workers are more productive, and their increased earnings may make them more viable consumers). This dynamic has taken a sinister turn in the African context. Patrick Bond of the University of KwaZulu-Natal suggests that the South African government's unwillingness to mobilize resources for public provision of ARVs fits with its embrace of market-oriented economic policies: AIDS 'is killing workers and low-income consumers' – largely expendable for purposes of macroeconomic policy – 'when South African elites in any case are adopting capital-intensive, export-oriented accumulation strategies.'[49] And private employers throughout the region are cutting their AIDS-related costs, for example by using pre-employment screening, outsourcing jobs, and restructuring employee benefits,[50] thus shrinking the size of the minority that has access to treatment and even rudimentary economic safety nets.

What is the alternative? Leaving basic needs to the unfettered marketplace represents a failure of both policy analysis and moral imagination. Needed, instead, is acknowledgment of obligations to protect health that cross national borders (and boundaries of other kinds), and a vision of development policy based on what the noted international relations and human rights scholar Richard Falk calls 'a regulatory framework for global market forces that is people-centred rather than capital-driven'.[51] Realistic prescriptions for improving health in the developing world must recognize that in the world as it now is, these guiding principles are mutually exclusive.

NOTES

1   United Nations AIDS Programme (UNAIDS) (2004) *2004 Report on the Global AIDS Epidemic: 4th global report*, UNAIDS, Geneva, p 193, <http://www.unaids.org/>.

2   Bates, Imelda et al. (2004) 'Vulnerability to malaria, tuberculosis, and HIV/AIDS infection and disease. Part 1: Determinants operating at individual and household level', *Lancet Infectious Diseases*, 4, pp 267–77.

3   Whitehead, Margaret, Dahlgren, Göran and Evans, Timothy (2001) 'Equity and health sector reforms: can low-income countries escape the medical poverty trap?' *The Lancet* 358, pp 833–6.

4   Russia is a recent G8 member, is not a major donor nation and does not participate in G7 finance ministers' meetings. Thus some of the commitments we examine are properly those of the G7, although for simplicity we refer simply to the G8.

5   G8 Communiqué, Okinawa (2000) Para. 26, 29–30. All official docu-

ments from G7/G8 summits and ministerial meetings are available on the website of the University of Toronto G8 Research Centre, <http://www.g7.utoronto.ca>.

6   Labonte. Ronald et al. (2004) *Fatal Indifference: The G8, Africa and global health*, University of Cape Town Press, Cape Town.

7   Population-weighted average calculated from World Bank figures at <http://devdata.worldbank.org/hnpstats/DCselection.asp>.

8   G8 Communiqué, Genoa, 2001, Para. 17.

9   Commission on Macroeconomics and Health (2001) *Macroeconomics and Health: Investing in health for economic development*, WHO, Geneva, p 11, <http://www.cid.harvard.edu/cidcmh/CMHReport.pdf>.

10 Ibid., Table A2.6, all figures in constant 2002 US dollars.

11 Michaud, Catherine (2003) *Development Assistance for Health (DAH): Recent trends and resource allocation*, prepared for Second Consultation, Commission on Macroeconomics and Health, 29–30 October, WHO, Geneva,
    <www.who.int/entity/macrohealth/events/health_for_poor/en/ dah_trends_nov10.pdf>.

12 G8 Communiqué, Genoa, 2001, p 15.

13 Figures from Global Fund website,
    <http://www.theglobalfund.org/en/funds_raised/pledges/>, accessed 4 September 2004.

14 Global Fund (2004) *Global Fund Observer (GFO) Newsletter*, 26 (June), <http://www.aidspan.org/gfo/archives/newsletter>.

15 Langley, Alison (2004) 'African AIDS drug plan faces collapse', *Observer*, 14 March.

16 Anema, Aranka et al. (2004) 'Is "3 by 5" enough? Recalculating the global need for antiretroviral treatment', letter, *The Lancet*, 364, pp 1034–5.

17 Padarath, A et al. (2003) *Health Personnel in Southern Africa: Confronting maldistribution and brain drain*, Equinet Discussion Paper 3, Equinet, Harare,
    <http://216.198.233.143/tbx/docs/
    Padarath%20et%20al.%20-%20Medact-HST-Equinet.pdf>;
    Huddart, J and Picazo, O (2003) *The Health Sector Human Resource Crisis in Africa*, Bureau for Africa, Office of Sustainable Development, US Agency for International Development, Washington DC, <http://www.aed.org/publications/HR_IssuesPaper.pdf>.

18 Dugger, Celia (2004) 'An exodus of African nurses puts infants and the ill in peril', *New York Times*, 12 July.

19   Schrecker, Ted and Labonte, Ronald (2004) 'Taming the 'brain drain': a challenge for public health systems in southern Africa', *International Journal of Occupational and Environmental Health*, 10, pp 409–15.

20   McCoy, David (2003) *Health Sector Responses to HIV/AIDS and Treatment Access in Southern Africa: Addressing equity*, Equinet Discussion Paper 10, Equinet, Harare,
      <http://www.equinetafrica.org/bibl/docs/DIS10AIDS.pdf>.

21   NEPAD (2002) *Health Strategy*, NEPAD Secretariat, Pretoria.

22   See for example Creese, A and Kutzin, J (1967) 'Lessons from cost recovery in health', in C Colclough (ed.), *Marketizing Education and Health in Developing Countries: Miracle or mirage*, Oxford University Press, Oxford, pp 37–62; Gilson, Lucy (1997) 'The lessons of user fee experience in Africa', *Health Policy and Planning*, 12, pp 273–85; Wadee, Haroon et al. (2003) *Health Care Inequity in South Africa and the Public/Private Mix*, Work in progress on the RUIG/UNRISD project *Le défi social du développement:* Globalisation, inequality and health care, University of Geneva, Geneva,
      <www.unige.ch/iued/new/recherche/ruig-dsd/docs/SAN-SA-01.pdf>.

23   Quoted in Mill, J E and Anarfi, J K (2002) 'HIV risk environment for Ghanaian women: challenges to prevention', *Social Science and Medicine*, 54, p 331.

24   Schoepf, Brooke G, Schoepf, Claude and Millen, Joyce V (2000) 'Theoretical therapies, remote remedies: SAPs and the political ecology of poverty and health in Africa', in Jim Yong Kim et al. (eds), *Dying for Growth: Global inequality and the health of the poor*, Common Courage Press, Monroe, Maine, pp 91–126.

25   Baker, Dean and Chatani, Noriko (2002) *Promoting Good Ideas on Drugs: Are patents the best way? The relative efficiency of patent and public support for bio-medical research*, Center for Economic Policy Research, Washington DC, October,
      <http://www.haiweb.org/campaign/access/TACDpresentations/deanbaker-arepatentsbestway.pdf>;
      and generally Health Action International <http://www.haiweb.org>.

26   Sell, Susan K (2003) *Private Power, Public Law: The globalization of intellectual property rights*, Cambridge Studies in International Relations, Cambridge University Press, Cambridge, p 96.

27   Galvao, J (2002) 'Access to antiretroviral drugs in Brazil', *The Lancet*, 360, pp 1862–5.

28   Declaration on the TRIPS Agreement and Public Health (2001) WTO,

Geneva, Para. 2, <http://www.wto.org/english/thewto_e/minist_e/min01_e/mindecl_trips_e.pdf>.

29 'Implementation of paragraph 6 of the Doha Declaration on the TRIPS Agreement and public health', Decision of the General Council of 30 August 2003, WTO, Geneva,
<http://www.wto.org/english/tratop_e/trips_e/implem_para6_e.htm>.

30 Orbinski, James (2004) 'Access to medicines and global health: will Canada lead or flounder?' *Canadian Medical Association Journal,* 170, pp 224–6; Elliot, Richard (2004) 'Canada's new patent bill provides a basis for improvement', *Bridges Monthly Review,* 8:5, pp 19–20.

31 Médecins sans Frontières (2003) 'Access to Medicines at the WTO: countries must save lives before celebrating success', press release, 11 September, http://www.accessmed-msf.org/prod/
publications.asp?scntid=12920039472&contenttype=PARA&>.

32 Global Forum for Health Research (2004) *The 10/90 Report on Health Research, 2003–2004*, Global Forum, Geneva , p 112,
<http://www.globalforumhealth.org/pages/index.asp>.

33 Kennedy, Peter G E (2004) 'Human African trypanosomiasis of the CNS: current issues and challenges', *Journal of Clinical Investigation,* 113, pp 496–504.

34 Trouiller, Patrice et al. (2002) 'Drug development for neglected diseases: a deficient market and a public-health policy failure', *The Lancet,* 359, pp 2188–94.

35 Walgate, Robert (2004) 'G8 support for vaccine initiative draws mixed reactions', *The Lancet,* 363, p 2055.

36 Schoepf, Brooke G (1998) 'Inscribing the body politic: AIDS in Africa', in M Lock and P Kaufert (eds), *Pragmatic Women and Body Politics,* Cambridge University Press, Cambridge, p 111.

37 Piot, Peter (2004) 'Plenary address for closing ceremony', 15th International AIDS Conference: Getting ahead of the epidemic, Bangkok, 16 July, UNAIDS, Geneva, <http://www.unaids.org/>.

38 Cornia, Giovanni Andrea, Jolly, Richard and Stewart, Frances (eds) (1987) *Adjustment With a Human Face, vol. 1: Protecting the Vulnerable and Promoting Growth*, Clarendon Press, Oxford.

39 See for example Bijlmakers, L A , Bassett, M T and Sanders, D M (1998) *Socioeconomic Stress, Health and Child Nutritional Status in Zimbabwe at a Time of Economic Structural Adjustment: A three-year longitudinal study*, Research Report 105, Nordic Africa Institute, Uppsala,
<http://130.238.24.99/webbshop/epubl/rr/rr105.pdf>; Bassett, M T,

Bijlmakers, L A and Sanders, D M (2000) 'Experiencing structural adjustment in urban and rural households of Zimbabwe', in M Turshen (ed.), *African Women's Health*, Africa World Press, Trenton, NJ, pp 167–91; Breman, Anna and Shelton, Carolyn (2001) *Structural Adjustment and Health: A literature review of the debate, its role-players and presented empirical evidence*, Working Paper WG6, p 6, Commission on Macroeconomics and Health, Cambridge, Mass.

40   Hanlon, Joseph (2000) 'How much debt must be cancelled?' *Journal of International Development*, 12, pp 877–901; Pettifor, Ann and Greenhill, Romilly (2002) *Debt Relief and the Millennium Development Goals*, United Nations Development Programme, Human Development Report Office, New York, December.

41   Cheru, Fantu (2001) *The Highly Indebted Poor Countries (HIPC) Initiative: A human rights assessment of the Poverty Reduction Strategy Papers (PRSP)*, E/CN.4/2001/56, United Nations Economic and Social Council, Geneva, <http://www.unhchr.ch/Huridocda/Huridoca.nsf/0/d3b348546ad5fb91c1256a110056aca4/$FILE/G0110184.pdf>; Labonte et al., *Fatal Indifference*, pp 26–9.

42   Brock, Karen and McGee, Rosemary (2004) *Mapping Trade Policy: Understanding the challenges of civil society participation*, IDS Working Paper 225, Institute for Development Studies, Brighton, p 20, <http://www.ids.ac.uk/ids/bookshop/wp/wp225.pdf>.

43   G8 Communiqué, Genoa, 2001, Para. 3.

44   Chang, Ha-Joon (2002) *Kicking Away the Ladder: Development strategy in historical perspective*, Anthem Press, London.

45   Webb, Michael (2000) 'The Group of Seven and political management of the global economy', in R Stubbs and G Underhill (eds), *Political Economy and the Changing Global Order*, 2nd edn, Oxford University Press Canada, Don Mills, Ontario, pp 141–51.

46   Wysocki, Bernard (1995) 'The outlook: foreigners find U.S. a good place to invest', *Wall Street Journal*, 7 August.

47   G7 Communiqué, Cologne, 1999, Para. 13.

48   Ibid., Para. 20.

49   Bond, Patrick (2001) *Against Global Apartheid: South Africa meets the World Bank, IMF and international finance,* University of Cape Town Press, Cape Town, pp 179–82.

50   Rosen, Sydney and Simon, Jonathon L (2003) 'Shifting the burden: the

private sector's response to the AIDS epidemic in Africa', *Bulletin of the World Health Organization*, 81, pp 131–7.

51 Falk, Richard (1996) 'An inquiry into the political economy of world order', *New Political Economy*, 1, p 13.

15 Genoa 2001:
which side to be on?

Haidi Giuliani

I'm the mother of Carlo Giuliani, murdered by police in Genoa on 20 July 2001. My name is Adelaide Gaggio, Haidi for all those who know me. I'm 61 years old, and I'm a retired primary school teacher. I was born during the Second World War but I've never experienced hunger, fear, pain, destruction, violence – I've only come across them through stories told by relatives and friends, reading books, or looking at photos or films.

My father, a religious man, went off to the First World War at the age of 18, driving lorries full of munitions to the front line, and looked on politics with mistrust. But he handed down to his four children respect for justice, enthusiasm for work and a deep disdain for the puffed-up arrogance and lies of fascism. My mother taught us to love music, art, culture and the tranquillity of the wooded slopes of her Swiss mountains.

Since I was a girl it's been easy for me to decide which side to be on.

The first demonstrations I went to were anti-war: I supported little Vietnam, which was desperately fighting to free itself first from French colonialism, and then to defend itself from the terrible aggression of the United States. I lived through the years of exile from a military dictatorship with my Greek comrades, sharing their pain of the dictatorship's violence and illegality. And later I demonstrated against the violence and injustice of Pinochet's dictatorship in Chile.

So wars and dictatorships have punctuated many years of my life, and they were always caused by a few individuals' lust for power, the interests of big business and forced importation of an economic system. You can take your pick from South America and Central America, black ghettoes in the United States, apartheid South Africa, China after Mao, the disintegration of the Soviet colossus, tribal wars in Africa, Tibet, Palestine, Chechnya, ex-Yugoslavia, Afghanistan.... You can't live as if the rest of the world doesn't exist. When my children grew up, they also chose which side to be on.

In July 2001 a summit of the 'big eight' was held in Genoa – or rather, as someone once wrote, 'G1 + 7'. The city suffered a military invasion for this event; it was devastated and raped. The old town, one of the biggest and most densely populated in Europe, was separated from other areas and roads and houses – and therefore also from hospitals, shops, workplaces, life – by five-metre-high fences. Manhole covers were even soldered down, and public transport was diverted.

I believe this is already a sufficient reason for viewing that summit as madness, as regards where they decided to hold it and the kind of stage they decided to perform on. The 'big eight', with all their hangers-on, wanted – and still want – to carry on planning and deciding on the world economy, concentrating power and wealth in the hands of the West, in particular in the hands of the United States – condemning the South of the world to even greater poverty. They wanted, and still want, a free hand – no obstacles should stand in their path.

The reasons to oppose all of this were many, and were so important, such as the life of billions of human beings condemned to thirst, hunger, disease and war. How can you be indifferent and watch the devastation and destruction of the earth without even letting your own 'no' be heard, without trying to put a grain of sand in the wheels that are churning over the rights of entire people?

My son was murdered during the G8 summit in Genoa on 20 July 2001, as he tried – together with many young and not-so-young people – to stop violent police charges against assembly points and marches which were denouncing the summit's illegitimate nature, and were raising issues such as Third World debt, access to water, exploitation of natural resources and AIDS. This is the reason that has led to me raising my voice in opposition: I write and speak because I am Carlo Giuliani's mother. Even if my son's right to life hadn't been denied, I would still be sure that the only reason for the G8's existence is to cover the huge economic interests which daily deny the right to life of millions and millions of men, women and children.

I worked in a primary school for 35 years. When we used to talk with the children about right and duties we started from basic needs: food, a land where you live and work, the need for shelter and the possibility of protecting yourself from the rain and the cold and diseases. But we also spoke about the need to stick together, of learning and teaching yourself, of the right to freedom and peace. Very young people have an instinctive sense of justice – it's normal for them that everyone should have the same rights. But it's not so for those who govern us: the more responsibility people have, the less responsible they become. You just need to look around, even in our own countries which describe themselves as civilized and developed, even in many of our rich cities.

Every time I'm asked to express Carlo's point of view I answer that he should do it, that nobody has the right to speak for him. It's difficult for me to speak in his place: in a way it's like I'm betraying him. I don't think he'd want it: while his death belongs to everyone his life doesn't. However you could say he was a free spirit, who wanted to meet life face to face.

What speaks for him are his writings, his choices, his connections with his friends and the people who knew him. Carlo never said he wanted to become rich, he wasn't influenced by adverts, he didn't spend much on clothes. He preferred little Arab shops in the backstreets where he ate kebabs to McDonald's, where he never set foot. He definitely dreamed about travelling the world: he wanted to discover faraway countries, above all those in the South, starting perhaps with Palestine because he was strongly affected by the suffering of its people. This is why he had left university, and why after 'civilian military service'[1] with Amnesty International, he started work in order to save enough money for the trip. 'And what will you do afterwards?' I used to ask him. 'I'll manage,' he answered calmly. 'If you want you can always find a job, or somebody to share food with.'

Piero Sansonetti wrote in a book published a few months after Carlo's death:

> Is Carlo a hero? A martyr to be blessed? No – but why not? We're not at war, there are no martyrs, and the movement is definitely not a religion so it doesn't need either martyrs or saints. But Carlo is the symbol of an anarchic generation that has rebelled, in the political and existential forms it has created, with its activities and with its lifestyle. Why should we refuse this symbol, why must we 'attack' it, diminish it, criticize it? There is only one explanation: it scares us a bit.[2]

Yes, it's scary that a boy born in a privileged part of the world opposes the privileges that are offered to him, shows his disagreement, and refuses to be part of the system. But within the movement Carlo moves people, perhaps because he represents that part which all of us more or less keep hidden: he gets angry, he fights back, he opposes with courage a force which is much bigger than him, a blind and servile arrogance.

Not by chance, the police and the national media immediately invented, in opposition, the figure of the poor policeman younger than Carlo, terrified and under attack. They pretended he was alone and at the mercy of a group of rioters. They pretended to forget what had happened earlier: the provocations, the violence, the gunshots. They ignored the fact that the police ran over my son twice, threw stones at him, kicked him in the face as he was dying. Carlo's thin and youthful body, defenceless, probably moves people too. That blue balaclava wasn't a weapon, that roll of sellotape on his thin arm wasn't a weapon, the fire extinguisher that rolls to his feet and he picks up more than three metres away from the police Land Rover isn't a weapon – its only use was to try to disarm somebody who is threatening him with a gun. Even the photos provoked a debate, even those in which they tried to present him as a terrorist.

On the other hand, nowadays it's easy to be accused of terrorism. All that's needed is for you to disagree with your own government or with the current economic system to face accusations. The many activists currently facing trial in Italy know about this at first hand. And today we see so many men and women who fight for the independence of their country, who resist, being called terrorists, when only 60 years ago people would have called them partisans.

After all, is this not what Berlusconi always says? All you need to do is to keep on repeating a lie and it will sound like the truth. Just bung everything together: the twin towers and those who drive a car full of explosives at a tank; mix up attackers and the attacked, rights and injustices. People won't understand much, but they'll be frightened. And people who are frightened are no longer able to distinguish white from grey and grey from black, and are increasingly willing to be persuaded. More than that, they ask to be persuaded. For example, they ask to not have to think about children blown up by mines, one of Italy's biggest exports, not to think about the growing spread of the mafia, with which one minister has said 'We need to live'; the rickety boats full of people escaping from war and hunger, whom another minister has obtained the right to either repel immediately at sea, or send back to their country of origin – simultaneously condemning them to death and ripping up the Italian constitution.

Carlo unites the movement. In the square where he was killed, people of all ages come and leave something of their own experience: from schoolchildren to pensioners, people of different beliefs; from young communists, anarchists, Catholics, activists from social centres, those active in fair trade campaigns. Writers, poets and musicians have dedicated their work to him. Some party branches and social centres have been named after him; in the Venice region the disobedients have named a square after him. I'm sure if all these people met up together they'd have a lot to talk about, and they'd find a thousand reasons for divisions.

But Carlo creates unity, and there's a real need for unity! This doesn't mean fudging things, losing your own identity, cutting yourself off from maintaining your own views. It means establishing some common ground and working together from that. This was the great message of Genoa 2001. And in subsequent years the anti-war movement has shown that this can be done.

The right is monolithic in its common interest for money and power. It accepts hierarchical structures without any discussion, and is ferocious with those who fail: the boss always needs to be obeyed. The left isn't monolithic: it's got high ideals, that's why it's always discussing. In any event, I don't agree with any man – from the smallest to the biggest – who tries to get noticed within his group, in the newspapers, on television, using the method of criticism, attack, or murmuring insinuations or insults against those who are more visible than he is (and it's right to speak of males here). Who is it that keeps talking about 'splits' and 'divisions' within the movement? Perhaps those who have everything to gain from a weaker and more confused movement? Maybe those who are looking for their own space, for a higher profile?!

Too much damage has been done in the name of ideology. And above all the young, or those who are young inside, can't stand this any more. When I go around talking about Genoa 2001, about the trials currently taking place and the 'counter-trial' on Carlo's murder, which has been shelved without a trial, there are always tons of people and total unity. I've never heard a divisive word spoken by those who have got the interests of the movement, the earth and its peoples, at heart. Over the last few years Carlo has caused me to meet so many different people, both famous and unknown, really great people because their commitment, honesty and daily behaviour is great. I've met these people in the street, in social centres, in church cloisters or in party branches. We just need to be like them: roll our sleeves up and get to work, facing problems one by one and with determination, trying to solve them.

I wrote earlier that Berlusconi had institutionalized lying. But let's be clear about it: it's not as if before him nobody ever manipulated information. Yet he has shown that you can lie with impunity, that you can say something and then immediately deny it. He has encouraged ignorance and provided a platform for liars: in our country he hasn't simply gained control of the main media outlets, he has bought people's consciousness. This is the main reason that it is necessary and urgent to get rid of his regime and his 'throwaway' culture. I have not used the word 'regime' lightly. This is not only because Berlusconi has brought (post) fascists into government, or because of his conflict of interests – as somebody has already noted, we're in a regime when a prime minister forces through laws that place him above and beyond the law, when he frequently barges onto public television channels while he is speaking simultaneously on his own network, when the press and satirists are muzzled, and above all when journalists, politicians and intellectuals persist in underestimating him or pretend not to see what he is doing.

These are the reasons that I think it is pointless opposing Berlusconi if you don't expose and defeat 'Berlusconism' beforehand. This has infected everything: from television programmes to school curricula, it's a lifestyle, a way of viewing the world and relationships between people – even among many of his weaker opponents, when it's a question of their own personal conflict of interests. Even many committed comrades are not immune.

The anti-war movement has managed to unite a very broad front of organizations, associations, individuals; but we need to clarify what needs to be done to stop the war, and what we are willing to give up. Having established that peace is our greatest value, the basic right, without which all others lose their meaning, and having understood that either we all enjoy peace or nobody does, given that we're global citizens and don't live in a glass bubble, I think we all have to decide and behave accordingly and coherently. I think we need to give that word – peace – some content, make it something concrete on the basis of daily choices and acts, even minute ones. From when we get dressed in the morning, to when we get on a bus or a train or go shopping or when we're deciding where to go on holiday, we can all do this. Otherwise it will just be a word, a useless agglomeration of letters, and the Berlusconis of the world will continue to dominate.

Furthermore, we need to ask ourselves what it means to be for peace and against violence. I think we need to make an effort not to be hypocritical when we talk about violence: we shouldn't confuse the violence of those who attack with that of those who defend themselves, the violence of those who exploit and repress with that of those who oppose exploitation and repression. The partisans who fought fascism throughout Europe allowed all of us to live, yet they used violence. Let's try to remember this, and to not offend their memory with commemorations that verge on being false and hypocritical. But that kind of violence isn't enough today against weaponry which is so powerful. We know that because we see it. Yet let's not confuse resistance with terrorism, let's not jumble up those who blow themselves up because they've got no future, and those who hold meetings to decide upon the annihilation of entire peoples. We cannot bring about peace in this fashion, I'm absolutely certain.

Carlo rejected a consumer lifestyle; he refused to get a rung on the job ladder if it meant damaging others. And even if he was starving, he would never have put on a uniform. So here I am talking about him again, but as I've already said, he is the one who has given me a voice. I learnt this from Ebe de Bonafini, one of the courageous 'mothers of Plaza de Mayo',[3] who once said, 'Our children have given birth to us.' She once gave me a pendant that reproduces the headscarf these women wear, bearing the name of their 'disappeared' children. Although I really don't like badges or stickers I've worn it ever since because I feel that symbol represents me, I belong to it. There are so many of us it's impossible to count us.

Since then I've met many other mothers (and not only Latin Americans) in my wanderings to one city after another, remembering all the sons and daughters killed by the police in Italy, or cases in which the police, elements of the judiciary or the state have perverted the course of justice. I've begun to piece together the terribly long list of deaths that, just like Carlo's, have not found a word of truth or justice within a courthouse. The same thing has happened to those who died in the fascist massacres that bloodied our country during the 1970s. I've also met mothers of soldiers killed in peacetime, mothers of boys who have died in war, who today fight for the withdrawal of troops from the countries where their children were sent to 'bring democracy'.

When I was young I liked to sing. And although I don't sing any more, I still remember a song created from the words of the writer Italo Calvino, 'Where the vulture flies':

... A vulture went to a mother
but this mother said 'no!'
fly away vulture, fly away
I'll only give my sons to a beautiful girl
who takes them to her bed
I won't send them to kill
fly away vulture, fly away from my land ...

NOTES

Text translated by Tom Behan.
1   Military service was compulsory until recently in Italy. However the option existed to do 'civilian military service' even though you had to serve an extra six months.
2   Sansonetti, Piero (2002) *Dal '68 ai no-global*, Baldini and Castoldi, Milan, p 73.
3   These are the mothers of the '*desaparecidos*', the people 'disappeared' by the Argentinian military dictatorship of the 1970s, who for many years have held a weekly demonstration outside the presidential palace in Buenos Aires, demanding justice.

16 Where do we go from here?

Sam Ashman

The movement for global justice has come a long way since the Seattle protests at the World Trade Organization meeting in November 1999. In this chapter, activists, trade unionists, environmentalists and writers who are part of the movement in different ways, and in different continents, give their opinions about where we should go next. Most were interviewed at the third European Social Forum, held in London in October 2004.

RUDOLPH AMENGA-ETEGO

Founder of the Campaign Against Water Privatization, Ghana

One thing that is very clear is that we are facing a situation where corporate globalization is emerging as one phenomenon which is affecting all citizens all over the world. In Ghana, and in Africa generally, if you talk of forest degradation or the pollution of rivers through mining or water privatization – which deprives poor people of access to water – it is all about corporate greed. The way forward is for us also to act as one global citizen, to act as one people and unite all struggles, and then we can succeed. Corporations have a global reach, and the only way we can challenge them is to unite our struggles and meet them, in whichever part of the world they surface. Europe in particular has a key and fundamental role to play because most of these corporations happen to have their homes in Europe. Civil society in Europe must be bold enough to confront these corporations in their own backyards and to tell their governments enough is enough. They cannot continue to spend public money on promoting private greed. If we accept these are some of the things we need to do then I think the future is bright for civil society generally and for human rights globally.

PIERO BERNOCCHI

COBAS, confederation of rank and file union committees, Italy

We are trying to build around three goals. First we need to continue with big mobilizations against the war in Iraq. Second, and very importantly, we must mobilize against neo-liberalism in the field of social questions: attacks on pension rights, the privatization of schools, of health, the struggle against the general insecurity of work and for employment rights. Third, we must mobilize people in defence of migrants, against racism against migrants, and in defence of their rights. I think it is also important that we mobilize against the G8 in July. I hope we can organize a big mobilization. We must try. We discuss as a movement and this is very important, but we must also act.

JOHN PILGER

Writer and broadcaster

I think the obvious lies told by George Bush and Tony Blair over Iraq are nothing compared to the lies and the silences in our media. Take one example. The media reported how a Palestinian suicide bomber killed 16 Israelis in one town ending 'a relative peace and calm', a lull in the violence. What they didn't report was that during that 'lull' more than 400 Palestinians were killed. Seventy-one of them were assassinated and more than 73 of the dead were children. None of this was reported in the mainstream media as terrorism. And most of it was not reported at all.

Who dares identify Blair and Bush and their collaborators as war criminals? The embargo of Iraq had already taken the lives of a million people. It is one of the greatest crimes against humanity. We know Saddam Hussein had no weapons of mass destruction. That means Iraq was never in breach of the UN's resolutions and Bush and Blair know it. That means that the only people fighting legitimately in Iraq are the resistance groups defending their homeland. It means that 'our boys' are taking part in what the judges at Nuremberg called the paramount war crime: they invaded, unprovoked, a defenceless country. George Bush and Tony Blair appeared before television cameras at Camp David and cited a report from the UN's International Atomic Energy Agency alleging that Iraq was six months away from building a nuclear weapon. No such report existed but the media did not challenge it. The same thing is happening again: Iran is building nuclear weapons, we are told, but there is no evidence. What can we do? We can do a lot. The public is feared by great powers.

Independent journalists are feared by great powers. That's why governments mount propaganda campaigns. The millions

[210]

who marched against the war are feared by governments. We must never underestimate our power, and we must always be prepared for battle. There is a new consciousness, a new awareness across the world. That is what's good.

KEN LOACH

Film director, whose films include *Bread and Roses, Ae Fond Kiss, My Name Is Joe* and *Land and Freedom*

I think for us in Britain the most important thing is to build a political movement that brings together the anti-capitalists, the environmentalists, the socialists, the trade unionists and so on. We need that unity. We have it on our banners but we don't always abide by it. For me the best way to do this is to build Respect. I don't see another organization capable of doing it. Respect comes out of the anti-war movement and I think it's our best chance of bringing people together, and whatever misgivings people have, they should be inside. I think we should all join and make it work.

PAUL LAVERTY

Screen writer for *Bread and Roses, Ae Fond Kiss* and *My Name Is Joe*

I think the future is incredibly practical. We made a film, *Bread and Roses*, about cleaners up against multinational corporations against the backdrop of the Justice for Janitors campaign in the United States. It was a David and Goliath situation but what they did was incredible. They were illegal immigrants, easily threatened. Their bosses said, if you get involved in a trade union we will send you back to your own country.

Many of these workers had mortgaged their whole futures to cross borders and were sending money back home. To get people to organize when there is so much fear and intimidation is amazing. Justice for Janitors premised the campaign on the idea that you're not just fighting a union, you're fighting a whole community. They made contact with the bus users' union, low pay units, grassroots organizations, churches – both Catholic and Protestant – and students. The whole community were behind them. They blocked off roads, gave 'Turkey of the year' to the most exploitative organization, invaded expensive corporate offices. It was done with great panache and imaginative flair. We have to find creative ways to confront incredible economic power. A lot of people are determined to change their lives. We are talking about people with no health care, working double shifts, with three jobs. It happens in every single city in the world. In Canary Wharf in London cleaners are up against multinationals. People are right when they say we cannot live a dignified life in this way. We have to change it.

GLORIA INEZ RAMIREZ

National Executive, CUT trade union federation, Colombia

It is important for our movement to be united in order to give hope to people. Understanding different countries, and that there is resistance in many different countries, gives people the possibility to understand that another world is possible. In Colombia the state is trying to terrorize us into submission. But despite this, every day more and more people are becoming active, and more and more voices demand change, more and more voices are raising the demand for a society based on social justice and equality. It shows the spirit of the people cannot be crushed.

CHRIS NINEHAM
Globalise Resistance

The first thing is to grasp what the movement has already achieved. Across the world there is a crisis of legitimacy not just of the global institutions like the G8 and the WTO, but of the neo-liberal project itself. Who nowadays believes privatization works or that the war in Iraq is about making the world a safer place? This crisis has been created by the war and the social disasters of neo-liberalism but also by Seattle, Genoa, the uprisings in Latin America, the various Social Forums and the global demonstrations on 15 February. The great gatherings of the movement have symbolized new strength and new possibilities. They have had a huge global and local impact. That is why we are organizing the biggest broadest possible protest against the G8 at Gleneagles. But at the same time we need to think about new ways to broaden and deepen the movement, and how to score some strategic victories. The war on Iraq is the vicious cutting edge of globalization. That is why opposition to it has brought millions more onto the streets. The global movement linked to resistance in Iraq now has a chance of inflicting a defeat on the US Empire, a defeat that would have really dire consequences for the globalizers. In the heartlands of imperialism and beyond, this struggle has got to be our number one priority. I also think that trying to salvage relationships with ex-social democratic parties that have sold their souls to the market only holds us back. That means we can't give social liberals a free run in elections. It's very important that radical electoral alternatives are emerging out of the movement.

[213]

ALESSANDRA MECOZZI

FIOM, metal workers' union, Italy

We have a long way to go but we are still strong. I have hope and I believe in ourselves. Both the European and the World Social Forums have to continue but we also have to reflect on how we can better coordinate our policies. We have to take strength from the Social Forums but we must carry on organizing on different issues: war, racism, privatization, neo-liberal policies, workers' rights. We have to try to implement better policies. Today the most important issue is the struggle for peace and for social justice, and I really believe the two are impossible alone. We have to struggle for both of these at all the different levels. In every country we have to do this. We have to demonstrate against the war in Iraq and for the withdrawal of troops, and against the occupation of Palestine and for the destruction of the Israeli government's horrible wall but at the same time we want another, social, Europe – a Europe for workers and for migrants.

JOHN HOLLOWAY

Professor of Political Science, Mexico, and author of *Change the World Without Taking Power*

Capitalism is a disaster for humanity and we urgently need radical social change. We do not know how such a change can take place. We have ideas but no certainties. That is why we must have discussions, respecting the differences, but recognizing we are all part of the same movement. How should we go on? Should we focus our struggles on the state or should we turn our backs on the state as far as we can? I argue we should turn our backs on the state as far as possible. If we focus our struggle on the state it pulls us in a certain direction: it separates our struggle from society to a struggle on behalf of society, it pulls us into a process of reconciliation with reality, with capitalism.

The concept of betrayal comes up over and over again. Leaders betray not because they are bad but because the state separates leaders from the movement. We need forms of organization that articulate what we want, council or communal organizations. We need invention and experimentation in our push to self-determination. The state pushes against this. When I say the state, I include parties. Parties reproduce the state form. The party is not the right way to organize. I am not saying that we should not cooperate with some, or that struggles that take another route are to be condemned, but that parties exclude: they impose hierarchies; they weaken and bureaucratize the anarchic effervescence of the struggle for self-determination at the heart of the movement.

How do we move against and beyond the state? If we do not make capitalism tomorrow then it will not exist. We make it, and we have to stop making it. We have to refuse, to break time, continuity and history. Refusal is the key concept when we think of alternatives to the state and the creation of a new world. There is no model, just a multiplicity of struggles and experiences. We must construct our own power to make a different world.

ORONTO DOUGLAS

Environmental Rights Action, Nigeria

The key here is solidarity. We need to understand what is happening elsewhere in the world. We need to be able to draw dotted lines and connections from one community to another and be able see the way forward in terms of localized struggles for global solutions. We must also look very critically at whether the current drivers of the world economy have the moral right to do so. I'm talking about corporations, big governments and big institutions. Take the World Bank for example. It was set up to abolish poverty. Fifty years on, what has it done about poverty? Poverty has become democratized. There are more poor people all over the world than 50 years ago. If an institution has not fulfilled its mission you should dismantle it and set up an alternative.

Corporations have become empires. What do you do with empires? You dismantle empires because they don't work! We should break down these corporations, not allow more mergers and acquisitions. Corporate culture does not work well for the environment, for ordinary people or for society. Oil is underneath my village and my community in Nigeria. The village is still wretched, the water is polluted, the forest has been vandalized, and of course wars revolve around resources. Why is the world pushed to war at the moment? Because of oil, the major energy driver. We are saying that we must stop that sort of driving force, based on taking resources that don't belong to you because you have power, because you have a bigger voice. We must refuse to be involved. We must work together, and find solidarity.

LES LEVIDOW

London Social Forum

The G8 and the international financial institutions continue to promote a capitalist model of development, especially for agriculture. We need to analyse these capitalist strategies. They are about enclosing the commons of many kinds, and turning more and more land into capital, through the international division of labour and through free trade. It's not just about privatizing seeds and subordinating farmers' knowledge to laboratory knowledge. We have to analyse resistances and alternatives to that agenda so we can support non-capitalist and anti-capitalist alternatives. The anti-capitalist movement may be limited by the assumption that the state and/or the market are the basic alternatives we face. We need to go beyond those limitations by identifying informal types of commons, resources that provide the means to resist the capitalist work discipline and marketization. We need to identify informal communities that sustain those commons, and then to think strategically about how these experiences can be extended into more spheres of life, as a way to make another world possible. In this way we can undermine their policies, and move beyond simply criticizing their policies.

ALEX CALLINICOS

Professor of Politics at the University of York and author of *An Anti-Capitalist Manifesto*

The international movement for another globalization continues both to grow in size and to become more radical. In 2004 the World Social Forum in Bombay and the European Social Forum in London were both successful events, but they were also pervaded by an anti-imperialist politics focused on resisting the occupation of Iraq, which went beyond anything seen in previous Forums. The challenge facing us is how to maintain this momentum.

One factor that complicates the task of addressing this is that, as the radicalization has grown, sharper divergences have developed between left and right within the movement. Moreover, some of the features that developed in the earliest stages of the movement are becoming obstacles to further progress.

The formal exclusion of political parties from Social Forums makes very little sense when the movement is helping to give birth to new political alternatives to social liberalism such as Respect in England. Nevertheless, I am very confident that we can successfully address these problems.

The G8 summit at Gleneagles is a particularly important focus, in part because the other side are trying to use it to regroup ideologically. Look, for example, at Tony Blair's and Gordon Brown's attempt to project themselves as Africa's best friends at the rich man's table. In fact their remedies amount to yet more of the free-market policies that have wrought such devastation on the continent. For the G8 we have to present a convincing critique of these false solutions and to demonstrate that our movement is the real ally of the peoples of the Global South in the North.

KATE HUDSON

Chair of the Campaign for Nuclear Disarmament

Unity of the movements against neo-liberalism and war is crucial to the advance of the cause of peace and social justice. Neo-liberalism and war are two sides of the same coin of US global domination, which together bring impoverishment to the majority of the world's population and death to countless thousands of innocent civilians. The United States has its sights on other countries that do not comply with its political and economic goals, and there will be attempts at further wars, which may well include the use of nuclear weapons. Understanding this relationship is fundamental to any advance. Clarity of analysis is vital to ensure our strategies are sound: then above all we need unity of our movements, making the links and working together in the broadest possible way. We have done this over the past three years in the anti-war movement, nationally and globally. Let's continue – and expand – this approach through to the G8 and beyond.

MEENA MENON
Mill Workers' Action Committee, India

The G8 is a good chance for Great Britain! Wherever they are, we should be there. It is not the G8 countries versus the G20 countries as some now say. To me, it is a question of putting people's policies against the policies of the G8. It's about putting a people's agenda against the elite agenda of the G8 – the rapacious, profit-oriented agenda of the G8. It is not poor countries versus rich countries any more. The neo-liberal globalization politics of the G8 marginalize and create poverty in both the North and the South. We have to stop them at every step. There can be no soft talking any more. It is too big. Seattle and Cancun have set the framework, and they should suffer the same fate in Scotland.

A number of key themes emerge from these interviews that suggest 'where we go from here':

- The necessity of international solidarity, and of building links between different struggles.
- The importance of continuing opposition to the war in Iraq, and of support for the Palestinians.
- The importance of opposition to neo-liberal social policies and to corporate power in general.
- To continue with the World and European Social Forums as important arenas for debate, building links and organizing.
- To continue to mobilize, in particular against the G8 when it meets in Scotland.

[219]

Conclusion:
Naming the problem

David Miller and Gill Hubbard

Everyone, even the most die-hard defender of the established order, recognizes that we face serious global social and environmental problems. The news media regularly circulate the latest figures on the latest social problems: the country with the worst pollution, highest infant mortality, lowest life expectancy, epidemic rates of drug abuse, poverty, anti-social behaviour. But the mainstream media, popular debate and elite discussion treat these – at best – as a procession of seemingly unrelated and inexplicable facts and events. At worst, the tendency is to suggest that whatever the problem – racism, obesity, unemployment, famine, war – the people affected are in some way culpable. If in doubt, blame the victim.

Either way, the context necessary to understand the problem and how it is caused is invariably missing. To paint in the context requires that we show how apparently isolated social facts are linked causally to other social facts; that they are not so isolated after all.

Take the example of the city of Glasgow, where we both live. Glasgow is the biggest city in Scotland, the media capital of the country, but not its financial or political capital. Glasgow is known throughout the United Kingdom, and beyond, for a whole series of social problems. The news adds to the list every few days: record levels of heart disease, high smoking rates, low levels of confidence and self-esteem, the highest poverty and deprivation, the lowest life expectancy. Glasgow has the three poorest constituencies in Britain. In the poorest, Shettleston, according to the Child Poverty Action Group, life expectancy for men is now 63. This is '14 years less than the national average ... nearly 18 months shorter than a decade ago – Britain's first reduction in lifespan since the Second World War'. Life expectancy in Shettleston is on a par with that in occupied Iraq.[1]

Glasgow's problems are often reported with a perpetually renewed sense of amazement on the news. If the newscaster gets over his or her surprise, the next recourse is to find someone to blame. First on the list of usual suspects are the people of Glasgow themselves. They smoke too much, won't eat healthy food, are politically apathetic, lack the get up and go of more entrepreneurial cities. Occasionally the spotlight turns on the government (the Scottish Executive in Scotland). But there is no routine link made between the latest statistic and the system of power that runs Britain. No one, not even an 'expert' commentator, says, 'This morning another report of the dire social circumstances in Glasgow further illustrates the problems of neo-liberal capitalism.' As the novelist J G Ballard notes, the lesson of any serious account of how Britain works is that the people themselves, even Parliament, royalty or civil service, are not in charge. 'Money rules, and the City dominates our lives, with a little help from the Prime Minister and the media.'[2]

The problem, in other words, is capitalism. If we widen the focus from Glasgow or any of the former industrial towns of Britain to the global picture, we find similar links. From Cape Town to Chiapas, from Cochabamba to East Timor, there are the same problems. It is capitalism as a social system that unites the questions of debt and corporate power, of war and food security, of racism and privatization, of poverty and health. All around the world the same issues face humanity.

SOCIAL MOVEMENTS FOR GLOBAL CAPITALISM

How did we get here? How did the successive waves of free market reforms, privatization and liberalization come about? Globalization did not just pop out, new-born, from the womb of the structural power of capitalism, as some on the left seem to assume. On the contrary, every ruling class 'is compelled, merely in order to carry through its aim, to represent its interest as the common interest of all the members of society ... it has to give its ideas the form of universality, and represent them as the only rational, universally valid ones.'[3]

As it was in 1845, when these words were written by Karl Marx, so it is today. Part of the strategy of today's ruling class is to present globalization as unstoppable. 'Globalisation is not just inevitable – though it is that – it is a good thing', as Blair has put it.[4] Blair's account leaves out the fact that 'Globalization ... is thought out, organised, managed, promoted, and defended against its opponents by identifiable groups of people working in identifiable organisations.'[5] Or as Corporate Watch put it, 'the earth is not dying it is being killed and the people who are doing it have names and addresses' (Utah Phillips).[6]

One name above all is associated with the killing of the earth and of its people. All over the world the name of George W Bush lives in infamy as the agent of destruction of the environment and of Iraq. The story of how the neo-conservative activists associated with the Project for a New American Century (and other think-tanks and lobby groups) took control of the machinery of US government is well known. What it tells us about great power is the necessity for change to be organized and fought for. The neo-con victory was the result of a long process of political activism and organization.[7] The neo-cons themselves can be quite unselfconscious about their aim to change the whole basis of world affairs, as one senior Bush adviser explained to the US journalist Ron Suskind:

> The aide said that guys like me were 'in what we call the reality-based community', which he defined as people who 'believe that solutions emerge from your judicious study of discernible reality'. 'That's not the way the world really works any more,' he continued. 'We're an empire now, and when we act, we create our own reality.... We're history's actors ... and you, all of you, will be left to just study what we do.'[8]

This calls attention to the collective hallucination of our rulers: the notion that they can float above the 'reality-based' world, even as they forcibly reshape it. But it also directs us to the lying, deception and propaganda, which put together are essential tools for the 'engineering of consent'. That phrase, coined by Edward Bernays in 1922, shows that the preoccupation of our rulers with managing public opinion is not new. But in the neo-liberal period, the techniques become ever more sophisticated and ever more desperate, as the gap between their rhetoric and 'reality-based' conceptions becomes ever wider.

This means that they have to invest more and more effort in constructing lies and propaganda, and we can certainly see that empirically in the past 20 years. Between 1979 and 1998 the UK public relations (PR) industry expanded more than elevenfold (in real terms).[9] In the United States the PR industry has become ever more important. Since 11 September 2001 the Bush and Blair propaganda machines have been overhauled and significantly expanded.[10] The neo-cons have not been alone in their political activism. Their networks tap straight into a very wide range of corporate funded think-tanks and front groups. The most well-known base of the neo-cons – the Project for a New American Century – has close ties with the American Enterprise Institute, itself funded by right-wing foundations and corporations such as Philip Morris and Exxon. Following the money in any direction takes you to the whole range of other corporate-funded groups and to corporate–state elite partnerships, networks and social clubs. Sometimes these organizations are deliberately shadowy, and cultivate a mystique, rendering their critics more liable to be dismissed as conspiracy theorists. But these organizations are not by themselves *the* conspiracy that runs the world. It is not this or that group that is in charge, it is the whole range of organizations working in a community of interest that makes up the global ruling class. So when we list and discuss these organizations below, we do so from the perspective that these groups, important though they may be, are not independently powerful, but powerful as expressions of global corporate and/or imperial interests. They are part of the social movement for global capitalism.

Elite networking groups like the British American Project for the Successor Generation are set up for particular purposes, and seem to function reasonably well in pursuance of those goals. The British American Project was set up to 'to perpetuate the close relationship between the United States and Britain' through 'transatlantic friendships and professional contacts' of the liberal elite. 'Five years before I joined BAP, I thought wealth creation and progressive politics were completely incompatible,' says Trevor Phillips, now Chair of the (UK) Commission for Racial Equality. 'BAP was one of the things that made me think that was absurd.'[11]

Pro-corporate think tanks, whether of the neo-con right or the third-way 'left', all engage in the same sort of projects and agendas. The Competitive Enterprise Institute, the International Policy Network, Demos, the Foreign Policy Centre (and hundreds of others) all play a role in the ideological battle over neo-liberalism.[12] Finally, and most importantly, peak business associations are at the forefront of lobbying to end regulation or beat back pressure for it. Peak business associations are not new, but they have taken on a new role under neo-liberalism. The involvement of transnational capital in politics is an undeniable tendency which has progressively strengthened across the globe. Everywhere you look, the denizens of the corporate interest conspire against democracy. In the European Union, the European Round Table of industrialists do their thing, while in the UN debate on the responsibilities of transnational corporations, the International Chamber of Commerce goes into bat. If the issue is the environment, the World Business Council for Sustainable Development rolls out the big guns. Wherever the spectre of regulation of business raises its head, there are business lobbyists engaged in conscientious struggle to defend their own interests.

THE END OF DEMOCRACY

Corporate front groups and elite policy networks are a means of protecting corporate interests from the risk of democratic decision making. All over the world, problems caused by capitalism reverberate: war, starvation, poverty, ill-health, pollution, access to clean water. Yet time and again corporate or imperial interests prevail, showing graphically the progressive destruction of democracy.

[225]

The techniques of 'manufacture of consent' are, Chomsky notes,

> most finely honed in the United States, a more advanced business-run society than its allies.... But the same concerns arise in Europe, as in the past, heightened by the fact that the European varieties of state capitalism have not yet progressed as far as the United States in eliminating labour unions and other impediments to rule by men (and occasionally women) of best quality, thus restricting politics to factions of the business party.[13]

Since 1991 (when these comments were written) the European Union and especially the United Kingdom have made great advances towards the US model. In the United Kingdom, the two main parties converged, and the United Kingdom has been at the forefront of globalizing free market reforms. Under 'New Labour' it is the United Kingdom (along with the far-right Spanish (under Aznar) and Italian governments) that has formed the vanguard of globalization in Europe. Meanwhile in Germany and France, where the trains occasionally still run on time, the restructuring lags somewhat.

The hollowing out of democracy under neo-liberalism works the same across the West. The result is that 'political apathy' becomes the watchword of the elite. Their takeover of the system provokes disengagement from their kind of politics. Chomsky notes that:

> By the early 1990s, after 15 years of a domestic version of structural adjustment, over 80% of the U.S. population had come to regard the democratic system as a sham, with business far too powerful, and the economy

as 'inherently unfair.' These are natural consequences of the specific design of 'market democracy' under business rule.[14]

The destruction of democracy has similar impacts in the United Kingdom. It is no surprise to learn that the lowest electoral turnouts in the United Kingdom almost precisely mirror the most deprived areas. The top three of the latter, as we noted above, are in Glasgow. Once again the apparently isolated statistics are actually connected. Is it any wonder that people are disengaged from formal politics, when they are comprehensively ignored and marginalized by the political system?

WHAT CAPITALISM DOES TO US: CONSUMERISM

The social movement for global capitalism is driven by the necessity to inculcate a consumerist ideology. Consumerism has spread from the over-developed nations of the West to the Global South, manufactured by transnationals (TNCs) and spread by the viruses of branding, marketing, advertising and public relations, pre-eminently via television. The cases of those countries that have only recently been introduced to the delights of consumer capitalism make the point most clearly. In Fiji, eating disorders were unheard of, until consumerism arrived with the introduction of television.

In 1995, the number of girls who self-induced vomiting to control their weight was zero. But three years after the introduction of television, that figure had reached 11%....The study showed that girls living in houses with a television set were three times more likely to show symptoms of eating disorders.[15]

According to Anne Becker, the Harvard nutritionist who conducted this study:

What I hope is that this isn't like the 19th century, when the British came to Fiji and brought the measles with them. It was a tremendous plague.... One could speculate that in the 20th century, television is another pathogen exporting Western images and values.[16]

In Bhutan, which introduced television only in 1999, the effect is even clearer. Within four years consumerism was taking hold:

There is something depressing about watching a society casting aside its unique character in favour of a Californian beach. Cable TV has created, with acute speed, a nation of hungry consumers from a kingdom that once acted collectively and spiritually. Bhutan's isolation has made the impact of television all the clearer.[17]

Without romanticizing Britain's past, these changing relationships between consumerism and culture bring home the extreme power of marketing and branding in the West, and the effects that this has on all of us. Branding and marketing continue to take children prisoner at younger and younger ages. The obsession with brands is the conscious result of corporate strategy. The marketers of cool operate everywhere to invade minds and bodies. Adele is nine years old. When she grows up she wants to be famous. Adele refers to people who don't wear branded clothes as 'nickynonames'. She would be wary about playing with such a person: 'I'd still be their friend, but I wouldn't hang around with them as much because.... You will get picked on for hanging out with a "nickynoname" person, so really you've got to be careful.'[18] Adele is, in marketing terms, a 'tween' (between 8 and 12), and is over the 'age of marketing consent'. Up a stage from here are 'teens', whose habits and desires are investigated and invested in by industry types known in the trade as 'cool hunters'. They search in the teen hangouts and convene focus groups of young adults, all the better to sell them with.[19]

Does all this consumer choice make us happy and contented? By any measure consumerist societies are now more discontented than in the past. The empirical evidence (on suicide, eating disorders, obesity, depression) is shocking but largely ignored.[20] When it is visible, the mainstream fails to note that the monster of consumerism is not the result of a few irresponsible marketeers, but is in fact the lifeblood of the capitalist system. If they can't make and sell more stuff that we don't need, the system would collapse.

There is no absolute relation between consumerist practice and pro-corporate values in the political arena. But is it any wonder that the addiction to the gear sold by the pushers of the consumer industries encroaches on the space for progressive politics?

FOR TODAY AND TOMORROW

We should not conclude from this that the struggle to save humanity and the planet is lost. The rulers of the world, the 'masters of the universe', are indeed in charge, and their power appears unassailable to many of us. But it is also clear that they are afraid of challenges to their power. We know this precisely because they spend so much time and effort – so much discussion, institutional and organizational activity – in attempting to combat challenges to their rule. Their intelligence services, their police, their propaganda, their advertising and marketing, their think-tanks, their lobbyists, their media, and yes, their military, are frantically busy trying to counter progress, peace and democracy. What are they afraid of? They fear the only other superpower on the planet: public opinion.

Or perhaps to be more precise, they fear the power of mobilized public opinion. For as things stand, public opinion the world over is ignored, marginalized, rebuffed, manipulated, smeared and excluded. But when it is mobilized, when as Shelley put it we 'rise, like lions after slumber in unvanquishable number', then concentrated power has a fight on its hands.

But already they don't have it all their own way. From Cochabamba in Bolivia where the privatization of the water system was reversed, to the resistance in Iraq, where the most powerful army in the world faces a myriad of daily attacks; from the ongoing process of resistance in Chavez's Venezuela, to the defeats of the World Trade Organization (WTO) in Cancun, they have a fight on their hands. The great movements of our era, the anti-war and global justice movements, have already shown that change is possible. All over the world neo-liberalism is being resisted. We don't often pause long enough to marvel at that phrase 'all over the world', but we should. For the first time in human history we are involved in a truly global struggle. This is an immense achievement. The movement of movements contains many views, demands and programmes for change, but we need to remember that it is only together that we will make another world come into existence.

The Annual G8 meeting, like the meetings of the WTO, the World Economic Forum and the rest, cannot now take place without the presence of demonstrators. We have driven them away from open politics to the 'retreats of the rich'.

They can run and they can hide, but they can't escape the reality of the disaster they have bequeathed humanity. As the polar ice caps melt, Iraq burns and millions live in hunger and poverty, the time for us to raise our voices ever louder is upon us. Let us do it together for humanity and for the planet, but above all for justice.

NOTES

1   McGarvie, Lindsay (2004) 'Scandal of our dying nation: sick joke', *Sunday Mail*, 7 March,
    <http://www.sundaymail.co.uk/news/content_objectid=14023777_meth od=full_siteid=86024_headline=-SCANDAL-OF-OUR-DYING-NATION—SICK-JOKE-name_page.html>.
    This is one more sense in which the Scottish squaddies from the poorest parts of Glasgow, now occupying Iraq, have more in common with the Iraqi people than with the government who sent them there.

2   Ballard, J G (2004) 'Seasons readings', *Guardian*, 5 December, discussing Anthony Barnett's *Who runs this place? The Anatomy of Britain in the 21st century.*

3   Marx, Karl (1845/1968) *The German Ideology*, Progress Publishers, <http://www.marxists.org/archive/marx/works/1845/ german-ideology/ch01b.htm#b3>.

4   Blair on Sustainability Summit: 'We can only face these challenges together' Prime Minister's speech on World Summit on Sustainable Development, Mozambique, 02 September 2002, British Embassy, Berlin, <http://www.britischebotschaft.de/en/news/items/020902.htm>.

5   Sklair, Leslie (2001) *Globalization: Capitalism and its alternatives*, Oxford University Press, Oxford, p x.

6   <http://www.corporatewatch.org.uk>.

7   Media Education Foundation (2004) *Hijacking Catastrophe: 9/11, fear and the selling of American empire*, <http://www.mediaed.org>.

8   Suskind, Ron (2004) 'Without a doubt', *New York Times*, 17 October, <http://www.nytimes.com/2004/10/17/magazine/17BUSH.html?ex=110 2222800&en=59b517c76fa3517d&ei=5070&oref=login&position=&or ef=login&pagewanted=print&position=>.

[231]

9   Miller, David and Dinan, William (2000) 'The rise of the PR industry in Britain 1979–1998', *European Journal of Communication*, 15:1, March, pp 5–35.

10 Miller, David (2004) 'The propaganda machine', in D Miller (ed.), *Tell Me Lies: Propaganda and media distortion in the attack on Iraq*, Pluto, London.

11 Beckett, Andy (2004) 'Friends in high places', *Guardian*, Saturday 6 November, <http://politics.guardian.co.uk/foreignaffairs/story/0,11538,1343704,00.html>.

12 For the best source of information on corporate front groups and think tanks see Disinfopedia, <http://www.disinfopedia.org>.

13 Chomsky, Noam (1991) *Deterring Democracy*, Verso, London, p 369, <http://www.zmag.org/chomsky/dd/dd-c12-s07.html>.

14 Chomsky, Noam (1997) *Market Democracy in a Neoliberal Order: Doctrines and reality*, Davie Lecture, University of Cape Town, May, <http://www.zmag.org/zmag/articles/chomksydavie.htm>.

15 BBC (2002) 'Television link to eating disorders', Friday 31 May, <http://news.bbc.co.uk/1/hi/health/2018900.stm>; Becker, A (2002) 'Eating behaviours and attitudes following prolonged exposure to television among ethnic Fijian adolescent girls', *British Journal of Psychiatry*, 180, June, pp 509–14.

16 BBC (1999) 'TV brings eating disorders to Fiji', Thursday 20 May, <http://news.bbc.co.uk/1/hi/health/347637.stm>.

17 Scott-Clark, Cathy and Levy, Adrian (2003) 'Fast forward into trouble', *Guardian Weekend*, 14 June, pp14–20, <http://www.guardian.co.uk/weekend/story/0,3605,975769,00.html>.

18 BBC (2004) 'Meet the tweens', *Panorama*, Sunday 21 November, <http://news.bbc.co.uk/1/hi/programmes/panorama/4011997.stm>.

19 Rushkoff, Douglas (2001) 'The merchants of cool', *Frontline*, PBS, 27 February, <http://www.pbs.org/wgbh/pages/frontline/shows/cool/etc/script.html>.

20 James, Oliver (1999) *Britain on the Couch*, Arrow, London.

Contributors

Sam Ashman is a member of the editorial boards of *Historical Materialism* <http://www.brill.nl/m_catalogue_sub6_idl7936.htm> and *International Socialism* <http://www.swp.org.uk/ISJ/ISJ.HTM>.

Tom Behan is the author of *Dario Fo: Revolutionary Theatre* (Pluto Press, 1999).

Noam Chomsky is one of the best-known writers on US imperialism. His most recent book is *Hegemony or Survival* (2004, Penguin) <http://www.chomsky.info>.

Vicki Clayton is National Co-ordinator of Jubilee Scotland <http://www.jubileescotland.org.uk>

Bob Crow is a former London Underground infrastructure worker and has been General Secretary of the National Union of Rail, Maritime and Transport Workers, RMT, since February 2002 <http://www.rmt.org.uk/>.

Mark Curtis is Director of the World Development Movement <http://www.wdm.org.uk>. His most recent books are *Unpeople: Britain's secret human rights abuses* (Vintage, 2004) and *Web of Deceit: Britain's real role in the world* (Vintage, 2003) <www.markcurtis.info>.

Susan George is Vice-President of ATTAC France <www.france.attac.org/>, Associate Director of the Transnational Institute in Amsterdam <http://www.tni.org/> and author of *Another World is Possible If ...* (Verso, 2004).

Lindsey German is convenor of the Stop the War Coalition, UK <http: //www.stopwar.org.uk/>.

Haidi Giuliani is the mother of Carlo Giuliani, murdered by police in Genoa on 20 July 2001 during the G8 Summit.

Olivier Hoedeman works with Corporate Europe Observatory (CEO), an Amsterdam-based research and campaign group targeting the threats to democracy, equity, social justice and the environment posed by the economic and political power of corporations and their lobby groups <http://www.corporateeurope.org/>.

Gill Hubbard is on the steering group of Globalise Resistance Scotland <http://www.grscotland.net> and helped to set up G8 Alternatives in Scotland <http://www.g8alternatives.org.uk>.

Ronald Labonte is Canada Research Chair on Contemporary Globalization and Health Equity, University of Ottawa, Canada. He is co-author of *Fatal Indifference: The G8, Africa and global health* (University of Cape Town Press, 2004) and 'What's politics got to do with it? Health, the G8, and the global economy', in *Globalisation and Health*, ed. I Kawachi and S Wamala (Oxford University Press, forthcoming).

Colin Leys is emeritus professor of politics at Queen's University, Canada. His most recent books are *Market Driven Politics* (Verso, 2001) and (with Susan Brown) *Histories of Namibia:*

Living through the liberation struggle (Merlin, 2005). He is co-editor of *Socialist Register* <http://www.yorku.ca/socreg/>.

Caroline Lucas was elected as one of the UK Green Party's first MEPs in 1999, and was re-elected in 2004. She is an associate of the International Forum on Globalisation, and has a long history of involvement in non-violent direct action and peace campaigning.<http://www.carolinelucasmep.org.uk/>.

David McCoy currently works as a public health physician in the United Kingdom. He has spent ten years working in South Africa as a clinician, researcher and health project manager, and is HIV/AIDS theme co-ordinator for the Southern African Network on Equity and Health (Equinet <http://www.equinetafrica.org>).

David Miller is Professor of Sociology at the University of Strathclyde, Glasgow, and the co-founder of Spin Watch <http://www.spinwatch.org>.

Emma Miller is the author of *Viewing the South: How globalisation and western television distort representations of the developing world* (Hampton, forthcoming). She is on the Scottish Steering Committee of the World Development Movement.

George Monbiot is a UK journalist and environmental campaigner. His most recent book is *The Age of Consent* (2003) <http://www.monbiot.com>.

Ted Schrecker is Senior Policy Researcher at the Institute of Population Health, University of Ottawa, Canada. He is co-author of *Fatal Indifference: The G8, Africa and global health* (University of Cape Town Press, 2004) and 'What's politics got to do with it? Health, the G8, and the global economy', in *Globalisation and Health*, ed. I Kawachi and S Wamala (Oxford University Press, forthcoming).

Tommy Sheridan is one of the best-known Members of the Scottish Parliament. He is a member of the Scottish Socialist Party <http://www.scottishsocialistparty.org/>.

Michael Woodin was, at the time of his tragically early death in 2004, aged just 38, Principal Speaker of the Green Party of England and Wales. He was elected as Oxford's first Green City Councillor in 1994, and was one of the city's most respected politicians. He lectured in Psychology at Balliol College, Oxford, and wrote and broadcast widely.

Salma Yaqoob is a chairperson of Birmingham Stop the War Coalition and on the national executive of Respect <http://www.respectcoalition.org/>.

Index